JOSEPH THE SILENT

Michel Gasnier O.P.

JOSEPH THE SILENT

SCEPTER

London   Princeton
Nairobi   New Delhi

This edition of *Joseph the Silent* is published:
in England by Scepter (U.K.) Ltd., 21 Hinton Avenue, Hounslow TW4 6AP; e-mail: general@scepter.demon.co.uk;
in the United States by Scepter Publishers Inc., P. O. Box 1270, Princeton, NJ 08542; e-mail: general@scepterpub.org;
in Kenya by Scepter Ltd., P. O. Box 28176, Nairobi; e-mail: focus@users.africaonline.co.ke;
in India by Scepter, P. O. Box 4009, New Delhi 110 017.

This is a translation of *Trente Visites à Joseph le Silencieux*, Paris, 1960.
With ecclesiastical approval

ISBN 0 906138 49 3
© Original – Michel Gasnier, 1960
© Translation – P.J. Kenedy & Sons, New York, 1962
© This edition – Scepter (U.K.) Ltd., 2000

Cover: *The Two Trinities*, Bartolomé Esteban Murillo (1617-1682), Trustees of The National Gallery, London.
Translated by Jane Wynne Saul, R.S.C.J..
Cover design consultant: Michelle Pinto & Associates; typeset by MI Intermedia, and printed in Singapore.

Contents

Author's Preface (to the first edition)

The Gospels tell us very little about St Joseph, and that little in very few words. Suddenly he appears. Nothing is said of his birth, his early life. His death is not mentioned. No words of his are recorded. It would be a great mistake, however, to measure his greatness, the role he was to play in the designs of God, by the few allusions made to him in the New Testament.

The Gospels are never very wordy. In fact, very little mention is made of the Blessed Virgin. Only what is essential is touched on and that is strictly concerned with the mystery of the Incarnation. It is up to us to mine the Scriptures to bring to the surface the treasures they contain. Those texts that relate to Joseph are heavy with hidden meaning. The details they give, sparse as they are, when meditated upon, become suffused with light. They enable us to form a true, finely drawn, attractive portrait, so that this life so obscure, so withdrawn, appears before us alive and gripping. The darkness, which at first sight seems to hide even the bare outlines, suddenly shines with radiant light. The more the few texts are studied, the more faithfully they are meditated upon, the more glorious the hidden truths are proved to be, the greater, the more beautiful the revelation.

To make up for the reticence of Holy Scripture, this book on St Joseph has been written in the same spirit as that of a former work – *Thirty Visits to our Lady of Nazareth*. It is an attempt to reconstruct the historicity of St Joseph's life, and to be called at the same time a study of his spirituality. Here he is called "the Silent" to emphasize a most attractive personal characteristic.

The question might be asked whether or not this is a work of the imagination only. The answer is, "Certainly not!" It follows as closely as possible the Gospel record and is in line with the teachings of the Church. On the other hand, it draws considerable support from the meditations and conclusions of the Fathers of the Church, the Doctors, theologians and hagiographers.

Reference has also been made to extra-biblical and contemporary sources which help to place the development of the saint's life in its geographical and historical background. "That period," as Daniel-Rops so rightly says, "in which the early years of the Virgin were passed, in which the miraculous event of the Annunciation and the birth of her son took place, is one of the best known in ancient history." Thanks to Flavius Joseph and the Talmud, both of which give us so much information on the customs of the Israelites of that epoch, it is rather easy to write with precise knowledge about what was probably the daily life of a pious and law-abiding Jew of that time.

It is the author's hope that these pages may increase devotion to him whom the Church does all in her power to exalt according to the measure in which he sought to efface himself.

We might repeat what St Teresa wrote on this subject: "I do not remember ever having asked anything of St Joseph that he did not grant me, nor can I think without wonder of the graces God has given me through his intercession, nor of the dangers of soul or body from which he has delivered me. It seems to me that God grants to other saints the power to help us in such and such a need. But I know by experience that St Joseph helps us in every need, as if our Lord wanted us to understand that, as He himself was subject to him on earth because there he held the place of a father and was called by that name, now in heaven He can refuse him nothing."

In poetic language, Francis Jammes continues St Teresa's thought when he says: "O my dear ones, I promise you that he who goes about like one of the common herd, like one of us, with his tools on his shoulder and a smile in his beard ... he will never abandon you."

Publisher's Note (to this edition)

After Michel Gasnier's ordination as a Dominican priest, he carried out his ministry in Paris for some 25 years. He was then appointed Director of the Dominican retreat house adjoining the famous monastery of Le Saulchoir. There this scriptural scholar was still able to produce over twenty books on biblical and theological subjects. Père Gasnier died on 1 July 1964.

Since the first edition of this book there have been a number of notable developments which Père Gasnier would doubtless have included in a revised edition of this work. When Pope John XXIII closed the first session of the Second Vatican Council he announced that the name of St Joseph was going to be included in the Roman Canon of the Mass. In that conciliar gathering, which represented the whole Church brought together in the Holy Spirit, there was proclaimed the great supernatural value of St Joseph's life, the value of an ordinary life of work done in God's presence and in total fulfilment of his will.

In August 1989 to mark the centenary of Pope Leo XIII's Encyclical Letter on St Joseph, Pope John Paul II promulgated his Apostolic Exhortation *Redemptoris Custos*, on the person and mission of St Joseph in the life of Christ and of the Church.

1

Joseph prefigured
in the Old Testament

Can we find such another like him in whom is the spirit of God? (Gen 41:38)

Generations of Christians are conscious of the exceptional part played by Joseph in the mystery of the Incarnation. Knowing that the Old Testament foretells and announces the New, they have busied themselves in searching out, in the history of God's people, for those signs and prophecies that might prefigure the virginal father of Jesus.

Certain personages, closely resembling Joseph in their mission or in their virtues, have caught their attention.

They see, for instance, in the patriarch Noah who drew into the ark the dove bearing the green olive branch in her beak as a sign the rains had ceased, an image of Joseph, guardian of Mary, that mystic dove who, in bearing Jesus Christ, would bring salvation to the world.

In Eliezer also, that faithful servant of Isaac's family, charged with watching over the bride of his master, they see the figure of him to whom was confided the guardian ship of the Virgin-Mother.

Again, it is of Joseph they think on reading those texts concerning Moses which describe him as the meekest of men, the intimate friend to whom God had confided all his secret designs.

In David, too, in the eyes of many interpreters, the person of Joseph is seen: "He is truly the son of David, a son not unworthy of his father," writes St Bernard. "He is the son of David in all the strength of that term, not by the flesh so much as by his faith and holiness and loving reverence, for God looked upon him as another David, well able to guard his secrets."[1]

But if we have good reason to find in the Old Testament prophetic announcements of St Joseph, it is most especially true in the person who bears the same name, the son of Jacob. Pope Pius IX in his 1870 decree proclaiming Joseph patron of the Universal Church, and Pope Leo XIII in the famous encyclical, *Quanquam Pluries*, of August 15, 1889, which echoed a great number of the Church Fathers and the Liturgy itself, make the statement formally.

Not only do they bear the same name–that merely points the way–but in their virtues and in their lives are found to an astonishing degree the same warp and woof of trials and joys. Each one–both just men in the full meaning of the word–each one devoted himself soul and body to the mission assigned to him, dreading only that any honour which

---

[1] Homily II on the *Missus est*

belonged to his Master might be attributed to his servant.

Both Josephs, by a chain of providential circumstances, were led into Egypt. The first, harried by his brothers' fierce jealousy, was a figure of the treason wreaked on Christ. The other, fleeing from the wicked fury of Herod, followed a like path into exile to save him who was to be the pure grain of the elect.

To the older Joseph, God gave the gift of being able to interpret dreams and thus foretell his own destiny. The later Joseph, too, received in dreams the directions God wished him to follow.

It might seem as if the dreams of the first Joseph, though verified in his own person, received their perfect realization only in the mission of the second. Here is what the Book of Genesis tells us of the former:

"Now Joseph had a dream, and when he told it to his brothers, they hated him the more. He said to them, 'Listen to this dream I had. We were binding sheaves in the field; my sheaf rose up and remained standing, while your sheaves gathered round and bowed down to my sheaf.' His brothers answered, 'Are you to be our king? Are you to rule over us?' And because of his dreams and words they hated him the more.

He had another dream which he also told to his brothers. 'I had another dream,' he said. 'The sun, the moon and eleven stars were worshipping me.' When he told that to his father and his brothers, his father reproved him. 'What is this dream that you have had?' he said. 'Can it be that I and your mother and your brothers will come to bow to the ground before you?'" (Gen 37:5-10).

Those dreams were fulfilled in the life of the first patriarch when his father with all his family came to Egypt and prostrated themselves before him who had become the viceroy of the country, the provider for all peoples on the earth. It is right and just for us to think that the dream of the first Joseph prefigured that mystery of Nazareth which would astonish the world when Jesus, the Sun of Justice, and Mary, praised in the Liturgy for her spotlessness and beauty, would place themselves under the authority of Joseph, the head of the family. And later also, the whole assembly of saints would clap their hands to acclaim the merits of him who had made himself the servant of the Word Incarnate.

The first Joseph won the confidence and favour of Pharaoh. He became the keeper of the granaries of Egypt, and, at a later time when a frightful famine laid waste the land, he was able to bring about a reign of prosperity and abundance. Pharaoh, marvelling at the wisdom of his steward, soon made him governor of his kingdom, and to all who came to him crying for food, he said: "Go to Joseph and do what he tells you."

So, too, the second Joseph was charged with providing bread for the family at Nazareth, and later he was to be given the mission, as Leo XIII wrote, "to safeguard the Christian religion, to be the titular defender of the Church which is truly the house of the Lord and the Kingdom of God on earth."

When the Bible recounts that Pharaoh took the signet ring from his finger and placed it on Joseph's, clothed him in fine linen and put a golden chain around his neck, mounted him in his chariot while heralds cried out before him, "bow down", must we not see in this the prophecy of the triumph of our own most glorious Joseph? And it is the Church which applies to him the command once given by Pharaoh: "Go to Joseph. Put yourself under his protection. Have confidence in his wisdom and power!"

Another virtue common to both completes the touching parallel–chastity. The first Joseph recoiled from the vile suggestions of Potiphar's wife, saying: "My master ... Has put all that he owns in my care. Nor has he withheld a single thing from me, except yourself, because you are his wife. How then can I commit this great crime, and sin against God?" Mad with resentment, the wretched woman falsely accused him to her husband, and Joseph was cast into prison– a place he preferred to the commission of sin.

Even more perfect was the chastity of the second Joseph, who not only refrained from any sinful action but knowing that God's chosen possession, the most perfect of creatures, the spouse of the Holy Spirit, was placed in his care, preserved boundless respect and veneration for her.

It is not really necessary to leaf further through the Bible to find other figures or images or symbols of the Spouse of Mary, though there are many more: Joseph as guardian of that garden of Paradise, the fruitful ground of the Virgin's womb, where the tree of life grew....

There is the Ark of the Covenant which God commanded Moses to cover with pure gold (Exod 25:17). The two cherubim surmounting the "propitiatory" turned ever toward each other–their golden wings spread out, adoring, protecting, interceding–were a fitting image of one whose prayer mounted ever to the Lord and was ever heard. The two cherubim might also symbolize Mary and Joseph bending over the crib in Bethlehem where lay Jesus, victim and propitiation for our sins.

God had ordered Moses to hang a veil of fine linen, woven in hyacinth and purple and scarlet yarns, before the Ark of the Testament, so as to shield it from the gaze of the profane. This veil, too, may be thought of as an image of Joseph, himself an object of honour and respect, who by his presence alone imposed on others reverence for Mary, and guarded the secret of the virginal Incarnation.

It goes without saying that the Holy Spirit willed none of these figures to be taken absolutely, but each may be thought of as fittingly applied to St Joseph's mission. No one need hesitate to make use of the imagery of the Old Testament to envisage him–as will be done all through this book–as the watchful guardian of the new earthly Paradise, the protecting angel and adorer of the Incarnate Word, the veil beneath which the Eternal Trinity carried on its most sublime and most fruitful work.

2

Ancestors of St Joseph

A man named Joseph, of the house of David
(Luke 1:27)

Before the birth of Jesus when the angel of the Lord appeared to Joseph in a dream, he addressed him by his title of nobility: "Joseph, Son of David". Two Evangelists, St Matthew and St Luke, give us Joseph's genealogy showing that he was indeed the legal descendant of David's royal line. The writers were able with little difficulty to get hold of documents to prove this since the Hebrews looked upon it as a sacred duty to preserve the lists of one's forefathers.

There was a permanent commission in the Temple whose business it was to examine and verify the genealogies of the priests and Levites. A legal obligation also made it necessary to be able to produce at any time proofs showing to which family a man belonged, the more so at a time of jubilee if claims were to be made for one's inheritance. The obligation was even stricter where the family of David was in question, because from that line the Messiah was to be born. It was therefore natural that Joseph and Mary should be most careful to safeguard their genealogical tables to prove that Jesus was indeed a lineal descendant of David.

That the Messiah was to be born of David's family was a point made very clear in the prophecies and no one had any doubts on the subject. "Whose son is the Messiah?" Jesus once asked of the Pharisees. "David's", they answered at once. And in fact it was a title by which he was often addressed: "Jesus, Son of David".

In naming the genealogical line of Joseph, both St Luke and St Matthew must have based themselves on what was written down in the tables by the notaries. Luke probably made use of the family archives kept at Nazareth, while Matthew seems to have consulted the official records of Bethlehem. Then, while Matthew puts his genealogical table at the beginning of his Gospel, showing Jesus' descent from Abraham down, Luke places his after the account of the baptism. His method is in the ascending form, tracing the line from the time at which he wrote back to Adam, the father of the human race. It strikes one at once how different the two lists are; only two names belong in both–Salathiel and Zorobabel.

In early Christian times the interpreters were worried about these divergences.[2] According to the testimony of St Jerome, these differences led to the denial by Julian the Apostate of the truth of the Evangelical writings. As a result, efforts were made to solve the difficulties.

Several hypotheses were proposed. From the

---

[2] See the letter of Julius Africanus to Aristides, cited by Eusebius (*Hist. eccles.* 1:7).

third century on, they cited the common custom of the Hebrews of using two genealogies–the natural and the legal. According to the levitic law, if a married man died without issue, his nearest relative was to marry the widow, and children born of that union were to bear the name of the deceased.

That would explain, for example, the two names given to the father of Joseph, called Heli by one, and Jacob by the other. The latter would imply that he had been the offspring of a levitic marriage. On the other hand, by the second marriage of his mother, Joseph's natural father would have been Heli, the legal right of fatherhood remaining to Jacob, the deceased father. This view seemed so genuinely sound that it was adopted by many Fathers of the Church.

According to another much later thesis, it is supposed that St Luke gave us the genealogy of Mary, and St Matthew that of Joseph. This easy explanation is attractive but it is in opposition to an authoritative text which cannot be contradicted.

Still another simple and very probable explanation may be offered. The Eastern conception of genealogies was by no means as exact as in our own day. We count only direct descendants; they were accustomed to include the collateral lines also. This left them much latitude in drawing up the genealogical tree. In going back to the rootstock, they passed over lateral branches to right and left and chose to mention only those most illustrious or holy. This latitude of choice could easily account for any apparent discrepancies.

When St Luke transcribed his own list, he was

perfectly aware of how St Matthew's differed from his. The fact did not trouble him at all, knowing as he did that he was perfectly within his rights, and custom would make him understood. He would probably have been much astonished had anyone suggested that his method might appear as a stumbling block to many in ages to come. In any case, both genealogies show Joseph as the last link in the chain before the birth of Jesus.

There may, of course, be room for surprise that we are given the genealogy of Joseph instead of that of Mary who bore him.

The answer is that among the Hebrews, the genealogy of women was never given, and the Evangelists in listing the one knew the other was included, since both came from the same stock and were closely related.

The two writers, however, were not insisting on this point. While affirming the virginity of Mary, they were also, according to the ideas of the time, stating officially Jesus' descent from the house of David, through Joseph. It was that, and only that, they saw in the legal genealogy of the Christ. Jesus was conceived and born of Mary when she was the wife of Joseph of the house of David; and for the Evangelists that was sufficient proof that Jesus was the son of David. They take pains to say "born of the Virgin Mary", thus insisting on her virginity. Joseph was appointed to protect the fruit of that virginity.

"If it could be proved," says St Augustine, "that Mary was not a descendant of David, it would be enough that the wedded husband was so descended, as that would suffice to make of the Christ, a lawful Son of David." [3]

Again, it is Augustine who writes: "Have no hesitation in tracing the lineage of Jesus to that line that was in Joseph, because in the same way in which he is virgin-spouse, he is likewise virgin-father. Do not be afraid of putting the husband before the wife according to God's and nature's laws.

Were we to put Joseph aside in order to speak only of Mary, he would be right if he said to us, 'Why do you separate me from my wife? Why do you not want the genealogy of Jesus to end with me?' Would we then say to him, 'Because you did not beget him in the flesh?' Again he would answer: 'But did Mary bear him only through the flesh? What the Holy Spirit wrought for her, he wrought for both of us.' " [4]

When we consider the forty generations enumerated in Joseph's genealogical table[5] we realize they cover two thousand years of history. It is said that all the glory, valour, faith and piety of that great people of Israel culminated in Jesus, the heir of the divine promises. It might also be said that if Joseph's ancestors bore the mark of a divine choice, they remained for all that very human. That patrician lineage was not

---

[3] *De Consensu Evangelistarum*, I, II, C. I, 17, 2.

[4] *Ibid.*

[5] The list given by St Matthew contains three series of 14 names each going from Abraham to David, from David to the Babylonian captivity, from the Babylonian captivity to the birth of Jesus. It is interesting to trace the parallel relationships. If each series comprised 14 names, it may be that 14 is a multiple of 7, a number held most sacred in the Old Testament. Besides, the Evangelist may have wished to call attention to the three great periods of Israel's history: the theocracy under the patriarchs and judges, the kingdoms, and lastly the priesthood.

made up of great and glorious names only. There were kings and shepherds, warriors and poets, builders and lowly nomads; among them we find illustrious names side by side with names scarcely known, saints, and four women far from irreproachable in their conduct.

We must see that Jesus who called himself "the Son of Man" and who had come to expiate men's sins, began his work with his own people, with that race from which he was descended, accepting his inheritance and taking his place as a true member of the human race. It was not merely to emphasize the contrast or bring into relief the difference between sin and sinlessness that three women who were sinners were mentioned among the ancestors of him whose name flames out shining as the rising sun. No. It was to bring out from the very first page of the Gospel that he who was born of Mary had come to save men and women, Jew and Gentile, just and sinner.

So Joseph, the final name on the list, is the key closing the Old Testament and opening the New. He appears in both Testaments. He is the last of the patriarchs of the Old and the first of the saints of the New.

And God, in being born into this world, chose as his father the heir of nineteen kings in order to teach kings that their blood carried with it a special responsibility. But this descendant of kings, who would never have thought of making anything of his noble origin, lived in poverty that the world might learn that in the kingdom of heaven poverty is the highest nobility, and, when accepted without lament, it will be a means of assuring a share in the riches of God.

3

Joseph of Nazareth

The angel Gabriel was sent from God to a town of Galilee called Nazareth (Luke 1:26)

We should be mistaken were we to imagine that Joseph, in spite of his humility and holiness, was not interested in the moral and spiritual heritage of his ancestors. The promises made to David and his descendants held too important a place in the Scriptures to be ignored. He felt himself to be one with those of his family who had gone before. He had a duty to be worthy of their virtues, to repair their faults, to be their witness before God by his very presence in the midst of that predestined race from which the Messiah was to come.

He never forgot where he was from. He called his forefathers to mind at times, not through pride but to remember each one to whom he owed a debt of gratitude. In his veins ran the blood of Abraham whose living faith and total obedience had won for him an everlasting posterity; the blood of Jesse of whom Isaias had said "a branch shall spring forth from his root." Many legal documents bore witness to the chain of generations by which he was linked to the prophet-king. Solomon was an ancestor glorious among rulers, whose wisdom was known to the ends of the earth, who had built the great temple in Jerusalem; Roboam, whose yoke the Ten Tribes had thrown off; Josaphat, the saint; Achaz, to whom Elias had foretold the virgin conception; Ezechias, brought back miraculously from the gates of death; Jechonias, the last of the Kings of Juda; Zorobabel, who had led the people home from captivity, and many, many more.

Could Joseph then, knowing he was the son of kings and prophets, of the royal blood of the illustrious tribe of Juda, could he then, especially after the extinction of the Machabees, not have realized that the crown was his by right? Yet, although he was a prince by birth, his status was that of an unassuming workman in a small town. Instead of living on the rich lands once owned by his tribe, he resided in Nazareth, an unpretentious village, among farmers and shepherds, a place of such small repute that the proverb, as the Evangelists tell us, ran: "Can any good come out of Nazareth?"

It was at Nazareth he became betrothed to Mary; we have reason to think that it was there also that he was born and spent his early years. Some commentators hold that he was born at Bethlehem, but in that case it would be hard to explain why, on his arrival there with Mary at the time of the census, no relative, no friend, no house was open to receive them and they were obliged to seek shelter in an inn.

Joseph at his circumcision, eight days after his birth, had received a name held in high honour among the Jews since Jacob's son, become governor under

Pharaoh, had made it illustrious. Doubtless his parents were sure that their son–the new Joseph–would render it more illustrious still.

Though the Gospels do not tell us so, the boy's parents must have taken him to the village school, connected with the synagogue, as was the custom, to be taught by the rabbis to read and write. Flavius Josephus maintains that because of their love for the Law many young Israelites attended the schools, if for no other reason than that later they might do the readings in the synagogues. On the other hand, since Joseph knew himself to be the descendant of David, he would have wished to be able to study the Scriptures concerning his lineage and especially those prophecies telling of the Messiah. This "just man" more than another would have longed to possess the science of that Law, the love of which was always food for his soul.

At twelve years of age, this boy had become like every faithful Jew "a son of the Law". From then on, in the eyes of God and men he was bound to be faithful to all its ritual obligations.

At that period a boy chose his profession. This was a double duty for Joseph, not only because he was poor and would have to earn his living but because the sacred traditions of Israel demanded it. The Jews–unlike the Romans–held manual labour in honour. It was looked upon as a means of calling down God's blessing. Every Jew–even if he were a rabbi or a possessor of great wealth–learned a trade and knew how to work with his hands.

Joseph chose to become a carpenter. Perhaps his father was a carpenter before him. Perhaps it was by personal preference. We simply do not know. In any case this occupation was to stand him in good stead when he opened his shop at Nazareth. We shall have to allude many times in the future to Joseph's trade. Here it is enough to say that though it was so unassuming, so humble, it was far from humiliating, and the carpenter-workman could look upon it as a badge of honour.

At Nazareth then, Joseph, without worldly goods or station, lived uncomplainingly by the work of his hands. Happier in his poverty than Augustus on the most powerful throne then in the world, he was more than content with his lot since it was God's will. The thought of Rome, conqueror of Jerusalem, the memory of the uprisings that had changed the face of his country had not disturbed his peace of soul.

Whenever he went to the synagogue, all he heard read, it is true, recalled the splendour of the surroundings in which his ancestors had lived. But on his return home there was in his heart no envy, no rancour, no longing for what had once been. He was not ashamed of his leather apron. He found no fault with Providence that had stripped his family of its worldly goods. When he journeyed to Jerusalem for the legal feasts and saw the evidence of its past glories, there was never even a thought of bitterness in his soul. Never parading his rightful titles before others nor trying to appear important, he was satisfied to be where God had placed him, to do what God asked of him with as much care and ardour as if he ruled a kingdom.

Poverty takes away nothing from true nobility. On the contrary, it adds to its lustre, as Jesus was to say years later in the Sermon on the Mount. Poverty indeed made of Joseph a privileged subject of the first Beatitude. If he was the son of David according to the flesh, he was more so in heart and mind. He was that "just man" of whom David, as he accompanied himself on the harp, had sung so long before.

Who were Joseph's relatives at Nazareth? Again, there are no documents to tell us. We have already said that according to St Matthew his father was called Jacob, and according to St Luke, Heli. This anomaly, as has been noted, may be explained as a result of a second marriage of his mother, or by the levitic law, by which one would be his natural, the other, his legal father. However, a certain historian called Hegesippus, who lived in Palestine at the beginning of the second century and who might have been able to follow up the traditions kept in the surroundings themselves, writes that Joseph had a brother named Cleophas. It is supposedly that Cleophas, an uncle of Jesus, who had married the Mary of whom the Gospel speaks as being the "sister" of the Virgin, and who was probably the mother of the four "brothers" of the Saviour–James, Joseph, Simon and Jude–and of three sisters whose names are not given.

The expression "brothers and sisters" of Jesus as used at that time is known to have meant first cousins. Such terms had in Bible usage a far broader significance than in our own language[6] for the simple reason that in Aramaic and Hebrew there was no word for "cousin", so the appellation "brothers" was used when any near relations were alluded to.

In the midst of his relatives in Nazareth, then, Joseph carried on his humble calling, occupied principally in pleasing God and keeping the Law.

He dressed like others who worked at the same trade. Like them–it was the custom–he carried a wood-shaving over his ear as a sign of his calling. His demeanour surely bore evidence of his nobility and holiness, and under his shabby clothing were found manners unusual in such surroundings. His attitude, his behaviour, his dignity, his calm–all would have commanded respect. On his face shone gentleness and goodness, in his eyes, truth and purity and understanding.

The villagers knew that here was one of David's line. Still, some–there are always some–because of his simplicity, his humility, his modesty that kept him from putting himself forward, his lowly trade, may have doubted or hesitated to believe in his noble origin.

It was indeed high time that God himself should come to earth to make known to man in what true greatness consists.

---

[6] So it is that Lot is called Abraham's brother though he was in fact his nephew. Laban was called the brother of Jacob though he was his uncle. The sons of Oziel and Aaron, the sons of Cis and the daughters of Eleazar were all written of as "brothers and sisters" though they were cousins only.

4

Joseph the carpenter

*From where has this man wisdom? Is he not the
carpenter's son?* (Matt 13:55)

In naming St Joseph's trade, the Evangelists, St
Matthew and St Mark, use a term whose general
meaning in Latin is artisan or workman.[7] Keeping to
that one meaning of the word, we could conclude that
St Joseph, as was customary in small towns, worked
in many capacities such as joiner, smith, mason,
potter, dyer, or any of the many trades which at that
time were in demand. The most ancient traditions,
however, are at one with the Apocrypha and with the
Fathers in calling Joseph *faber lignarius*, a worker in
wood, that is a joiner or carpenter.

It is true that St Hilary, St Bede the Venerable,[8]
and St Peter Chrysologus tell us he was a worker in
iron. St Ambrose and Theophilus of Antioch picture
him as cutting down trees, building houses. But none
of these occupations implies a contradiction. In a

---

[7] The word *faber* is common to *faber ferrarius*, smith, and *faber lignarius*,
carpenter.

[8] St Bede writes, "*Ferrum igne dominantem*", or one who shapes the iron after it
has been softened in the fire. St Isidore designates Joseph as *faber factore aeris*,
a worker in iron and other metals.

small village no labourer could be a specialist; the demand would not have been big enough for him to have earned a living. So Joseph devoted himself principally to working in wood as a joiner or carpenter. This would have obliged him at the same time to labour a little as a mason, a smith, or a woodcutter.

Some writers seem averse to admitting that Joseph could have worked at such jobs on the plea that "accompanied by great noise, they required much time and brute force; that they would have been completely out of harmony with the peace and quiet prayer of the Holy Family."[9] These are strange and rather shocking ideas. Surely if the God-Man came into the world to share the life of man, he would not have based his choice of profession on the condition that his eardrums be not offended nor his hands calloused.

The same want of understanding leads a few other authors to try to improve St Joseph's social position. According to them he should have been a contractor or architect in charge of workers inferior to himself–a prominent citizen of Nazareth. Such ideas would have made the Evangelists blush. From all that we know we must insist that Joseph was a little-known artisan in a small village, earning his livelihood in a quiet, hidden way, consonant in spirit with the mystery of the Incarnation with which he was so soon to be closely concerned.

---

[9] It is surprising to find among these Cardinal Lépicier whom we quote from his book *Saint Joseph, époux de la Tres Sainte Vierge* (Paris: Lethielleux, 1932).

In the second century, about A.D. 160, the philo-
sopher, St Justin Martyr, wrote: "Jesus was taken to
be the son of Joseph the carpenter, a carpenter in his
own right, among men making carts and yokes." St
Justin had been born in Samaria, at Neapolis, the
ancient Sichem, and was well able to gather information at firsthand from his Galilean neighbours.

In those days, as always, cart-wheels had hubs
of iron which the carpenter fashioned himself, thus
obliging him to add metal forging to his other work.
Even at the present time, Nazareth is still noted for
certain specialities–sickles, ploughshares, knives.
Joseph's trade is still very much alive in the place
where he had carried it on.

St Cyril of Jerusalem, who lived in the fourth
century, says that he had been shown a piece of wood
shaped like a roof gutter which was supposed to have
been carved by Jesus or his foster father.

It is a great temptation to answer yes to the
question posed by Maurice Brillant in his book *Le
Village de la Vierge* (The Virgin's Village): "Might
we use a familiar but telling phrase and say that Saint
Joseph in his little shop was a Jack-of-all-trades?"

He worked in wood and iron; he made furniture
and built houses. The villagers came to him when
they needed something mended, a door hung, a wall
strengthened, a lock replaced, a chest made or a tool
repaired. He shaped not only the thick planks needed
for supporting the mud or clay houses, but likewise
garden tools, cradles, biers. He made utensils for
housekeeping, stools, milk buckets, linen presses–

they had no use for clothes cupboards–and perhaps he did some fine cabinetwork. At Nazareth, for many of their needs the neighbours must have said to one another as Pharaoh of old, "Go to Joseph".

According to Eastern usage the shop was near or attached to his home. Like the smithies in our own villages, Joseph would have had an open shed in front of the shop, sometimes crowded with damaged carts, ploughs that needed overhauling, hewn logs lying on the ground, and cedar and sycamore tree-trunks leaning against the low roof for weathering. The Bible tells us what might have been found hanging inside on the walls of a carpenter's shop: a hatchet or two, saws, hammers, scrapers, compasses, jointers, mallets, drills, files.

Certainly Joseph was considered to be not only a fine workman noted for his skill, but a man of integrity. Everyone in the neighbourhood knew the work given to the carpenter would be carefully and conscientiously done.

He loved his trade. He knew it thoroughly from the ground up. He reverenced it in its relationship to the Law. Before God, work is not only a necessity; it calls for pride, nobility, a spirit of reparation. There is nothing slavish about it. On the contrary it is a kind of prayer, a way of finding God, a means of salvation.

To be a workman with these dispositions, to saw a log into planks, to fashion furniture is a joy. He enters his shop early in the morning, smells the forest odours in the wood, sees the sun caught in his tools. As an act of worship he prepares the day's work, dons his leather apron as a priest his vestment. Each gesture and movement he makes with love. It is with pleasure he serves his customers. He is proud, but without vanity, to give them of his best. He hopes that his earlier work has suited them, that the cart-wheel has held up, the doorframe not warped. Their satisfaction is his.

It is of Joseph we must think–as others have already mentioned[10]–when we recall the words of Péguy, writing of the days of his youth when "work seemed an incredible honour" and "men carved a chair with the same spirit and energy and warmheartedness with which they built cathedrals." Joseph gave to his carts and yokes the same care he would have given to a tabernacle, since he understood perfectly that a work done in love goes straight to God.

He never complained of his calloused hands, of the sweat he wiped from his brow. He sang at his work. He chanted to the rhythmic beat of his hammer the poem sung by his ancestor David:

'... praise [the Lord] with lyre and harp,

Praise him with timbrel and dance, praise him with strings and pipe.

Praise him with sounding cymbals, praise him with clanging cymbals.

Let everything that has breath praise the Lord!' (Ps 150:3-6)

Joseph's cymbal was a hatchet, his pipe a yardstick, his timbrel a plane, his harp a saw, his lyre a

---

[10] Especially Fr Bessieres in *Presence de Joseph* (Paris: Lethielleux, p. 51).

file. While he played on them his heart and soul were with God.

Never did the devil cross the threshold of that shop. Confounded and disarmed before this humble man, he could not understand such imperturbable defencelessness; he did not know on what side to attack, how to tempt. To attain his ends, the devil must find some trouble brewing, some spirit of discontent or revolt, the boast, "I will not serve."

This man of mystery seemed perfectly content to hollow out logs, to fashion cart-wheels. And Satan had to flee from the ring of Joseph's hammer, the sound of his saw. To him the sight of this "just man" was torture and frustration.

5

Joseph the Just

Joseph being a just man ... (Matt 1:19)

The evangelists' laconic panegyric of St Joseph strikes us, accustomed as we are to the use of superlatives and wordy phrases, as rather disconcerting. They state briefly, "He was a just man." However, that was no small praise. The word implies the fullness of sanctity. The justice here spoken of is not merely that virtue which consists in giving everyone his due; it is that sum of perfections which means complete union with and surrender to the will of God. In biblical language it is the union of all virtues. In the Old Testament the *just man* is the one whom the New Testament calls *the saint.*

Justice and holiness express the same reality. The portrait of the just man is drawn for us in the Psalms in a multitude of traits which depict the ideals of perfect moral rectitude God asks of men.

The just man is he who refrains from evil and does good; whose heart is pure; who is sinless in his intentions and conduct; who acts as is commanded toward God, his neighbour and himself. He does nothing without learning God's will. He praises him; he exalts him; he blesses his name; he trusts him absolutely and obeys him perfectly. He keeps his heart free from pride, ambition, desire for riches. He acts toward his neighbour with uprightness, honesty, loyalty. He has a horror of lying, duplicity, cheating. Toward all he is kind, generous and compassionate. To those in need he brings help, and practises the spiritual and corporal works of mercy as far as it lies in his power.

Blessed indeed is he, says the Psalmist over and over again, who acts thus. He will draw down upon himself God's divine good pleasure. Such a man is like a tree planted beside a stream, the leaves of which do not fade and which brings forth magnificent fruit in due season. Nonetheless he is not spared all trials, but in every one that falls upon him he sees the will of God and makes of them a means of spiritual advancement. And in the end he will receive a hundredfold.

Joseph's life was the true working out of this image. In every meaning of the term he was the *just man*. We must not be fooled by the fact that his picture in the Gospel is but dimly drawn. Though in the eyes of the World there is nothing striking, the truth breaks through the shadows and shows us a man of spiritual and moral grandeur, of true greatness in the sight of God. His praise was sung by Jesus in his prayer at the Last Supper: "I thank you, Father, Lord of heaven and earth, that you have hidden these things from the wise and understanding and revealed them to babes" (Matt 11:25; Luke 10:21).

Penetrated by divine grace, his heart was pure,

his will strong. Totally unaware of his own worth, he had a soul faithful and profound, open and straight-forward as a child's.

A just man. First with regard to God whom he sought to please in all things, to fail in nothing. He studied God's Law that he might conform himself to it in thought, desire, word and act. He sometimes had to stop his work to take a little rest. Those were the moments when he could retire to a corner in his workshop to read and re-read the songs of his fore-father, David. Then, back on the job, he would repeat the verses whose melody went up to God like sweet-smelling incense:

'Within my heart I treasure your promise, that I may not sin against you....

How sweet to my palate are your promises, sweeter than honey to my mouth' (Ps 118:11, 103).

'As the hind longs for the running waters, so my soul longs for you, O God.

Athirst is my soul for God, the living God' (Ps. 41:2-3).

'For you are my hope, O Lord; my trust, O God, from my youth....

... you are my strong refuge!

My mouth shall be filled with your praise,

with your glory day by day' (Ps 70:5, 7-8).

Joseph was not less the just man where men are concerned. He lived apart from all those matters which in Oriental countries are causes of unending disputes and arguments. At Nazareth, people knew that he did not talk much. He hated gossip; ill-natured talebearing he despised. All the same, he did not attempt to shut himself away from his neighbours, or seal himself up hermetically in his shop. His door was wide open, encouraging the passers-by to come in, to talk with him while he worked. His visitors were attracted by him. They were struck by his wisdom, his understanding, his sympathy. They felt better when they went on their way.

His professional honesty was well known. Because he gave to each man his due, they came to him to have their work done. He served them as quickly as possible, working sometimes late into the night, getting up early in the morning. His charges were never exorbitant, and yet, as all over the East, they tried to beat him down. Of course, they abused his kindness. They knew his reluctance to force payment, to go after those who refused to pay.

Joseph was of the same stamp as those just ones described by the Evangelists when they wrote of Simeon and Anna, the prophetess–both waiting for the redemption of Israel, for the fulfilment of the promises, longing with their whole hearts for the coming of the Messiah. Like them, he believed that the fullness of time, so often spoken of in the Scriptures, was near at hand. He had figured out that the seventy weeks of years which Gabriel had announced to David had passed, and that soon "He who was to come, would come."

Many Israelites, conscious of religious realities, had a presentiment that a new world was about to appear bringing with it "a golden age". Tacitus and

Suetonius have felt impelled to mention the rumour in their writings. In the soul of Joseph this hope burned with a bright flame, and his heart beat fast with boundless hope.

While others on the eve of that mysterious revelation gave themselves up to politico-religious speculations, he knew that the first need was prayer. With fervent desire he implored the Almighty that his hour might come quickly, that he would soon send him who was to bring light and salvation to the world.

Joseph little dreamed that his longings were to be fulfilled beyond his furthest hopes, that God had looked with mercy on this humble carpenter of Galilee, and that all generations would give him the title of Blessed. He did not know that he was himself the last of that long line of patriarchs leading up to the Messiah, and that to him, more privileged than the others, would be granted the grace of holding in his arms One whom kings and prophets had desired to see and hear, him of whom David on his harp in ages past had sung:

'... may your compassion quickly come to us, for we are brought very low.

Help us, O God our saviour, because of the glory of your name' (Ps 78:8-9).

'Rouse your power, and come to save us... if your face shine upon us, then we shall be safe' (Ps. 79:3, 20).

Joseph could never have even imagined that his person would be essential to the mystery of the Incarnation, that he would help to realize the designs of God in bringing joy to a world in anguish.

It was for that that God had made him the just man, fit for the greatness of his task. Whenever, say the theologians, God appoints anyone for a certain mission, he gives him the graces necessary to carry it out.

God had filled Joseph with wisdom, justice, holiness because he had predestined him to become the husband of Mary, the Mother of the Word Incarnate–the virginal father of Jesus.

6

Joseph the predestined

Our Father ... give us this day our daily bread
(Matt 6:11)

The souls of the just who lived before the coming of Christ, and who were familiar with the prophecies, were filled with immense hope. Knowing God was faithful to his promises, they awaited their realization. A Messiah was foretold whose mission would be to bring joy to the earth and save the world by freeing it from sin and the powers of evil.

Though none doubted this redemption would come, none could foresee how unexpectedly, according to human reason, it would be brought about. The Son of Man would appear among men not suddenly or strikingly, but despoiled of all the trappings of majesty. Unknown and humble he would come, a hidden life before a public life.

St Thomas,[11] seeking a cause for that obscurity, offers these principles. If the Eternal Word was to save the world through the Cross, a passible body was necessary. A glorious manifestation would have placed obstacles in the way of his plan: "For had they

---

[11] *Summa Theologica*, III, q. 36. a 1.

known it, they would never have crucified the Lord of glory" (1 Cor 2:8). On the other hand, his radiant splendour would have lessened the merit of faith; and, lastly, the reality of his human nature and his sufferings might have been doubted.

Had the Son of God no need to eat and drink and sleep, had he escaped all the ills inherent in human nature, the error of those who believe he became man only in appearance would have had some basis. He would indeed not have been the "Emmanuel" foretold by the prophets, God, one in nature with us, living with us and as we live.

All the same, however lowly the birth of the Man-God, in one point he was to be an exception: he was to be born of a Virgin. By the Holy Spirit he was to be conceived. Anything else we could not imagine. It would be unthinkable that the Son of God should have any but God for his Father in the exact meaning of the term. A prodigy doubtless, but a necessary one.

But what of the child's honour and the honour of his mother in the eyes of the world which knew nothing of the mystery? Would there not have been a baleful shadow darkening his way? Public contempt? Could such a stain have rested on him who had come to take away the sins of the world? Or on her through whom he had come?

"The virgin of whom he was to be born," as Isaias described her, could not cry from the rooftops the extraordinary favours she had received. Even though modesty, innocence, grace, purity shone on her countenance, in her actions, in her words, in her whole person, would anyone have believed her? Her statements would have been taken for shrewd dissimulations, and later on when the child of her flesh defied his hearers, "Which of you can convict me of sin?", they would have brought up contemptuously the manner of his birth.

God could, of course, have intervened to reveal the mystery of the virginal conception of his Son. A voice could have been heard as on Tabor to declare: "This is my beloved Son ... virgin-born." But such was not God's way. In his infinite wisdom he chooses to make use of ordinary and gracious means even when performing the greatest miracles. To protect the good name of his Son and his Son's mother, he is pleased to hide the mystery of this conception behind the veil of a holy and lawful marriage.

If a husband were necessary to safeguard the honour of the Virgin-Mother, he would also be needed to serve as the foster father of the child to be born. This seems a strange necessity when we consider that this child is the Word of God, the fostering father of all creation, on whom all things depend for life, subsistence, permanence, growth. Yet the role will be reversed and the creature will nourish the Creator. He who provides for all will ask help from a human being. Born like other infants–naked, fragile, weak– unable to provide the necessities his human condition requires, he will be able to make known his wants only by his infant cries and tears. And as near the cradle of every human child there should be found a father and a mother who will look after him with loving tenderness, feed and clothe him, so will it be here.

The Eternal Word in the midst of earthly trials, difficulties, dangers, will need an earthly protector, since his Father in heaven has left him defenceless. Neither soldiers nor angelic legions will be on hand to serve him; he will need a strong arm to shield and shelter him.

And it is to Joseph that these different functions are to be entrusted. In the beginning, when Adam was made from the dust of the earth, God's wisdom had declared: "It is not good for man to be alone; I will make him a helper like himself," and when the time had come for the sin of Adam and Eve to be repaired, God again saw that it was not good for the Virgin to be alone, without help, without support.

So God chose Joseph to fulfil his designs. It was Joseph who was predestined by Divine Wisdom to provide a hearth and home for mother and child that in the eyes of the world all things should be fitting. Guardian and defender, he would surround them with a cloistered wall of silence and simplicity to shield the innocence of Mary and the weakness of the child. Their honour, thanks to him, would be above suspicion. If challenged, the testimony of this witness of known integrity would be accepted.

As long as need be, until the child's identity should be revealed, Joseph's silent, holy presence would be enough to keep the Virgin's secret. For the time being his mission was to keep the mystery hidden from men. Later on only, the Apostles would be called upon to make known the mystery of God made Man.[12]

God's plans required further that Joseph take care of God's chosen ones in their days of trial and want and danger on their way to exile in Egypt. By the sweat of his brow he would earn their daily bread during Jesus' childhood and, when he grew older, initiate him into the trade he was to pursue for many years.

We must admit and wonder at Joseph as he fulfils the mighty task laid upon him. His to give the child who was the world's creator, a home; his to provide food and clothing for him who in his Providence feeds the beasts of the earth and the birds of the air, clothes the lilies of the field in garments fairer than those of Solomon. It is Joseph who takes the place of him to whom men pray: "Our Father, who art in heaven."

But though such high duties were imposed on Joseph, God asked of him something more: complete detachment. When God calls, his call requires that a man empty himself of self, that no will remain in him but the divine. Joseph's soul was ready for this stripping, this loss of all things. It was because of this that from all eternity God had chosen him, prepared him,

---

[12] St Ignatius of Antioch was of the opinion that this veil of secrecy was to hide the mystery from the demon himself. There was a widespread conviction, based on the Scriptures, that the devil did not know for certain that Jesus was the Son of God. This ignorance was explained by the fact that fallen intelligences were unable to penetrate the supernatural and the divine secrets, since God himself would call a halt for them at the entrance of the sanctuary.

fitted him spiritually for the lofty mission that would be his.

In the meantime, no one seeing this sandal-footed man walking along the narrow roads of Nazareth on his way to work with his toolbox on his shoulder could or would ever dream of his incomparable destiny. In their eyes and his own, he was a lowly, ordinary workingman. Yet it was he, Joseph, who by God's decree would make possible the Incarnation according to God's plan.

7

Joseph's betrothed

And the virgin's name was Mary (Luke 1:27)

Joseph, in his little shop at Nazareth, worked at his carpenter's trade; in his soul closely united to God, he was convinced that the long-awaited promises were about to be fulfilled. Over and over again he repeated the Prophet Isaias' prayer: "Drop down dew, O heavens, from above, and let the clouds rain on the just: let the earth be opened, and bud forth a saviour!"

Because the signs that announced the coming of the Messiah were appearing, all the righteous in Israel were praying ardently in the same words.

God had indeed already chosen in the humble village of Nazareth the one who was to give him to the world. "And the virgin's name was Mary."

She was the late-born fruit of Joachim's and Anna's union. Tradition holds that she had come in answer to their prayers and tears and penance. No great stir was caused by the birth of this girl-child whom all generations were to call "Blessed". To the eyes of the world there was nothing here out of the ordinary. She came, it seemed on the exterior, like other infants; but interiorly her soul was steeped in the perfection of holiness. At her conception she was dowered with the seven gifts of the Spirit, with no stain of original sin. The Liturgy dares to put on the lips of God himself this cry of admiration: "You are all fair; O Mary, pure, without blemish."

Tradition again tells us that she herself had asked that her early childhood be passed in the Temple that she might offer herself completely to the Lord. The early awakening of her intelligence owing to the graces she had received would have made this possible. Already she had understood that the highest wisdom for a human being is to surrender itself, soul and body, irrevocably, to the Lord God. She did not renounce love but on the contrary chose the first, the highest love; and to that love bound herself forever by the vow of virginity.

Though she knew she was of the family of David of whose line the Messiah would be born, though she longed as no other for the fulfilment of the promises, though she would collaborate with all her strength to bring about their realization, she thought herself entirely unworthy of sharing in their consummation. For this reason she offered up her sacrifice, praying that the hour of his coming might be hastened.

At that period, virginity, though held in honour by the Israelites, was seldom practised and in general proscribed by the Law.[13] The expectation of the

---

[13] This state, considered "exceptional", was practised by the Essena, as we learn from the scrolls discovered at Qumran. Though in theory they were allowed to marry, their religious fervour led them to prefer a celibate life.

Messiah so filled the people's minds that a refusal to marry seemed dishonourable as implying no desire to contribute to the coming of him who would restore the Kingdom of Israel. So the time came when Mary's relatives were to arrange a suitable marriage for her. She probably raised no objection, as she had told no one of the vow she had made; and, moreover, she was convinced that they could not understand and would not approve.

She left everything then to God, knowing that somehow he would clear up a situation at once so involved and so seemingly contradictory. She begged him to put in her path a man able to sympathize with, honour and respect her vow and willing that their union should be sealed only by a spiritual love.

These circumstances led to the building up of the legends found in the Apocrypha.[14] They have so gripped men's imaginations and been so tenaciously held to from generation to generation that they have come down to our own day, and it will be well to recall one or two. A famous one follows.

The High Priest, having summoned all the young men of the house of David who wished to marry Mary, ordered them to place their staves on the altar. He, whose staff would blossom miraculously, would be considered to be the suitor chosen by God. It was Joseph's rod, of course, that flowered.

Among those who took part in this ceremony

---

[14] Especially the Protevangel of St James the Less, The Gospel of the Nativity of the Blessed Virgin Mary, and The Gospel of the Infancy of the Saviour.

was a young man, very rich, very noble, named Agabus. His disappointment was so great that having broken his staff–Raphael has left us a famous painting, "The Espousals", of this scene–he fled into the desert for life.

The reality must have been much more simple and more easily imagined. It is generally believed that Mary's parents had died, and she had been placed in the care of the priest, Zachary. Her guardian told her one day–at the time such negotiations were carried on without consulting the girls–that he had been successful in finding a proper husband for her. He was called Joseph. His qualities were enlarged upon, especially the fact that he was of the house of David, the descendant of the kings of Juda, the most noble line of all. He was, it is true, a simple workman who earned his livelihood by the labour of his hands, but his profession was well thought of and in no way interfered with the practice of his religion. Moreover, he was looked upon as a man of integrity. He was honest, God-fearing, just.

When Mary learned she was to be affianced to Joseph, all her fears disappeared. She knew him well as he was of the same tribe, probably related to her. She had always admired his faith and the loftiness of his soul. She thought highly of this man whose hands were hardened by work but whose bearing was chaste and gentle, whose manner was serious and reserved.

On his side, Joseph had been struck by the mysterious loveliness of Mary. He saw in her face a flower-like purity. In her presence he was deeply moved by the conviction that here was some indefinable grandeur. He had thought the angels to be such as she.

Mary was obliged in any case, under pain of invalidating the marriage, to make known at their first meeting the vow she had taken. She did so quite simply. Later she was to speak with the same simplicity to the angel of the Annunciation.

She was sure that her words would sound an echo in the soul of this just man, and that he, like her, would choose the same manner of life. She knew she would receive from her future husband not merely acquiescence but the solemn assurance that her vow would be respected, that nothing would ever make him change this resolution.[15]

We can easily agree with the tradition held by the greatest number that Joseph, too, had made a vow of virginity and that in marrying, like Mary, he had but conformed to general custom. There is also another plausible explanation. Joseph had always led a life of perfect chastity.[16] What he had heard from the lips of this young girl had convinced him of the greatness and beauty of virginity and only increased

---

[15] St Thomas is of the opinion that before the marriage Mary had received a divine assurance that Joseph had the same dispositions as she (*IV Sentences*, Dist, XXX, q. II, art. 1).

[16] The opinion that Joseph had had a previous marriage–says *Le Dictionnaire de theologie* (article on Joseph)–was based entirely on the apocryphal *Protevangel of James*. In the first centuries of the Church there were a few Fathers of the Church in sympathy with this theory. Today it has been completely abandoned. The assumption that Joseph had children of this marriage, "the brothers of the Lord", runs up against too many diffficulties to make its acceptance possible.

his love and fervent attachment to that virtue.

After having explained to Mary that he could offer her only a modest home, he assured her that it was a great joy and privilege for him to have been chosen to take care of her, that he had promised God to remain as she, that he would always look after her as would a brother.

They both were filled with joy and exultation when, at the close of their meeting, each felt that their souls were joined in perfect accord. Mary's heart was flooded with peace and security, Joseph's with an immense desire to protect and cherish the precious gift confided to him. Descendant of kings, he had no court, no riches, no renown, but God had given him a treasure compared to which all the glory and wealth of Solomon were as dross and nothingness.

A text from the Book of Wisdom came to his mind to help him express in words his superabounding joy: "All good things have come to me together with her."

8

Marriage ceremony

Mary his mother had been betrothed to Joseph
(Matt 1:18)

Were any faith to be put in certain apocryphal writings,[17] we might think that Joseph was an old man when he married Mary. St Epiphanius was probably influenced by this idea when he unhesitatingly stated that Joseph had passed his eightieth year. Writers who accepted this theory were evidently trying to prove our Lady's perpetual virginity. Rather a detestable argument, since it attributed Joseph's continence to senility.

On the contrary, in those days as well as in our own, such an ill-assorted marriage would have been roundly condemned and looked upon almost as a profanation. Ordinary common sense demands that Joseph be in the flower of his age so that, on one side, the fatherhood of the child Jesus might be attributed to him, and that, on the other, he would be able to fulfil the duties of protector and foster father which God was to confide to him.

Custom in Israel required that young men be

---

[17] Especially *The Epistle attributed to St Jerome* and *The Gospel of the Infancy.*

married at eighteen or shortly after. Nothing obliges us to think that Joseph was older than others. Some documentary iconographs picture him as a beardless young man.[18] When later artists make him appear an old man, it is probably less in order to accent his age than to underline the perfection of his virtues, especially his prudence and maturity of character.

Certain authors have discussed whether or not he was good-looking. Their conclusions have usually been based on his prototype Joseph in the Old Testament, who was gracious of manner and agreeable to look upon. This could easily be admitted without declaring the argument settled. Certain it is that Mary would have looked rather to the moral character than to the physical attributes of her future husband.

Among the Jews the negotiations preceding a marriage were carried on more or less as a business affair. Endless discussions of the most minute details concerning both families were weighed in the balance. The betrothal of Mary and Joseph could not have escaped customary practice and must have proved a great trial to both of them.

No documents remain to tell us where the ceremonies took place—Jerusalem or Nazareth perhaps. All the relatives assembled. Though loving solitude, neither Mary nor Joseph tried to escape the usual gatherings, and since the ceremonies dated back

---

[18] In the catacombs of St Hippolytus in Rome he is thus pictured on a gravestone of the third century as also on the sarcophagus of St Celsus in Milan, which belongs to the fourth century.

to the times of the patriarchs, they were gone through with reverence and respect.

Joseph wore a long tunic over which a heavy cloak fell from his shoulders. As to Mary–the Cathedral of Chartres claims to be in possession of her garments given as relics in 877 by Charles the Bald who had himself received them from the imperial treasure house of Byzantium. The cloak is of beige-coloured material shot through with gold threads and hand-embroidered with white, blue and violet flowers.

Mary held out her hand to Joseph–not the delicate long-fingered hand painted by the Renaissance artists– but the hand of a good housekeeper who knew how to wash and mend and prepare a meal. He placed on her finger the gold ring symbol of union and possession, saying: "Here is the ring that unites you to me in the sight of God according to the Mosaic Rite."

He then handed his bride the written contract and a silver coin representing her dowry or marriage portion. Never had any bride placing her hand in that of her groom brought him the happiness that filled Joseph's heart at that moment.

From then on they belonged irrevocably to each other, for in Hebrew Law the betrothal was not a simple promise of marriage in the future, but, with binding force, was equivalent to it. In Deuteronomy, as in the Gospel, the betrothed was called "wife" because she was indeed that. Accused of infidelity, she would be obliged to suffer the punishment for adultery, and she would be stoned to death. Did her betrothed die, she would be looked upon as a widow. Nor could she be rejected except through the same process of divorce as the Law required for a married woman.

Cohabitation, however, was generally postponed for some months, perhaps a year. The rabbis held the bride should be given the time to prepare her trousseau, the groom, to fulfil the promises of the contract and prepare the home.

Actually, the betrothed could have marital relations and if the bride conceived a child by her groom, no fault would be found. Because of these facts, the endless controversies carried on later about Mary's conception of the Incarnate Word, some affirming that she was truly married, others denying it, are absolutely pointless—a mere war of words.

After their betrothal then, Mary and Joseph separated, each returning home to await the official marriage ceremony. From this time on, however, having made their irrevocable promises in the sight of God, they have become husband and wife in time and eternity. A secret agreement did indeed take away one of the purposes of marriage—renounced by their vows of virginity—the exercise of their conjugal rights.

This did not in any way alter the bond of union. Before God and man they were truly husband and wife, because the essential perfection of marriage was there. According to St Thomas: "It is the indissoluble union of souls, in virtue of which the spouses are bound to keep their fidelity inviolable."

They offered to God their virginity as a gift they

knew would be pleasing to him. They were far from guessing the results. They could not know that in renouncing the power to engender children according to nature, they were preparing themselves to receive the most sublime of favours. They did not know that their virginal union was the work of God, ordained by him as the means to bring to the world his Son, the Messiah.

The virginity of Mary was necessary to draw down the Word from heaven and make the Incarnation possible. Bossuet says: "As God fathered his Son in heaven by a virginal generation, so when he was to be born in time, a Virgin-Mother was needed." And because Joseph was to safeguard Mary's virginity, his own was not less necessary.

Here then are two virginal souls promising each other fidelity, a fidelity that would consist in both preserving their virginity. They have acted, it might seem, in a manner absolutely opposed to the hastening of the coming of the Redeemer. Yet for this very reason and for the value of their act, they have merited that God should place in the cradle of their virginal home a child, his only Son. On their own initiative they had signed the contract, made the promise which would prepare them for their unique, tremendous mission.

9

The Word made Flesh

Behold a virgin shall conceive, and bear a son
(Matt 1:23; Is 7:14)

Joy was never greater in any soul than that which sang in the soul of Joseph after his betrothal. He thought his happiness unique. Over and over he repeated those words of Holy Scripture, "Happy the husband that has a good wife, twice lengthened are his days" (Sir 26:1). "When one finds a worthy wife, her value is far beyond pearls" (Prov 31:10). His own lot was glorious. The thought of his bride never left him. He wore it as a seal upon his heart. Every day he seemed to love her more, and every day his gratitude to God for the gift he had received grew in like measure.

Let us beware of thinking that Mary's heart had remained unmindful of Joseph after she had made him her promise. As later she was to become the model for wives and mothers, so she will be the model of fiancées. She did not try to check her very real spontaneous love for Joseph. She looked forward to life in his home where charity and chastity would reign. With all her heart she thanked the Lord for having chosen for her so noble a companion, so sure a support. Each found in the other incomparable beauty of soul.

For the time being they lived in separate homes whose proximity permitted frequent visits. At each meeting the same light of confidence and understanding shone in their eyes. Their affection for each other was seen in the utter simplicity of their companionship.

While they waited to be united under the same roof, both were occupied in preparing for the future. Mary was busy with much sewing and spinning; Joseph had simple house furniture to make. Neither could guess that God was about to bring about the stupendous event that would dominate the history of the world. The exegetes, as has been noted, have much to say as to whether Mary and Joseph were to be looked upon as actually married or still, as the Gospel puts it, "espoused". The Gospel text leaves the matter open to discussion.

In either case, since both conditions conferred the same rights, before the Law Mary belonged to Joseph. Whatever might happen, the wife's honour would be preserved in the eyes of the world. In fact, congratulations would have been in order since fecundity was esteemed the joy and glory of the conjugal union.

The Angel Gabriel, it would seem, came as ambassador shortly after the betrothal. Springtime would have been chosen as a fitting symbol of earth's awakening from the long winter's night. The Liturgy places the feast in or near mid-March, and expresses its joy in the words of the Canticle:

'the rains are over and gone.

The flowers appear on the earth, ... and the song of the dove is heard in our land.

The fig tree puts forth its figs, and the vines, in bloom, give forth fragrance' (Cant 2:11-13).

The Gospel story need not be quoted. The words are locked in everyone's memory.

Mary is in her home. It is growing dark. She is saying her evening prayer. Suddenly the angel is there. "Hail, full of grace." He calms her fears and tells her that God has chosen her to bear the Messiah. Mary does not know the meaning of pride. She thinks only of the joy that is to come to the world and asks frankly, since she has vowed virginity, how this is to be done. The angel reassures her. The Holy Spirit will accomplish this work in her. Her virginity will not be lost. Knowing this, knowing that Divine Wisdom will bring it about, that human wisdom consists in submission to the will of God, Mary consents: "Behold the handmaid of the Lord; be it done to me according to thy word." And the Word takes flesh in her womb. The great mystery of love is consummated; Mary has become the tabernacle of God.

As if to guarantee the truth of his message, the angel tells her that in another home well-known to her, another miracle has taken place: "And behold, Elizabeth thy kinswoman also has conceived a son in her old age, and she who was called barren is now in her sixth month; for nothing shall be impossible with God" (Luke 1:36-37).

This news convinced Mary of what she should set about doing. Since God had given her a sign that the angel's message was true (she had had no misgivings on the subject), a visit to her cousin seemed to be indicated by him as an added proof. The child within her urged her on. The Messiah wished to sanctify his Precursor.

The day following the Annunciation when Joseph came to visit Mary, the only change he saw in her was an even greater sweetness in her manner, a more tender light in her eyes. An increased seriousness, too, he must have noticed. But Mary said nothing, gave not the slightest hint to let him know of the divine secret.

She did, however, express a desire to visit her cousin Elizabeth. She had but lately learned of her unexpected pregnancy and she was anxious to be of service to her. Joseph was surprised at her sudden request to undertake a journey of which, till then, there had been no mention, not even on the previous day, and his heart contracted at the thought of the separation the visit would entail. Yet convinced of Mary's wisdom, ready to accept any sacrifice that might be asked of him, and in order to prove his love and trust, he did not question her. In spite of the suffering her absence would cause him, he consented at once to her wishes.

Some commentators think Joseph accompanied Mary on the visit. Elizabeth, it is thought, lived at Hebron or Karim–today Ain-Karim–a five- or six-day journey on foot. How then could he have let her go alone, exposed to all the dangers on a bad road, ninety miles long, through inhospitable regions abounding in pitfalls and perils?

The objection cannot be answered, though the

Gospel implies that she went alone. We may be sure, however, that her faithful guardian saw to it that the journey would be made in safety. She might have joined some friend or relative, or a caravan of pilgrims on their way to Jerusalem to celebrate the Pasch.

What is certain is that he was not present at the meeting of the two cousins. Otherwise he would have heard Mary's *Magnificat* and learned about the mystery of the Incarnation which the angel only later revealed to him.

So Joseph's bride, hurriedly and wholeheartedly, started on her way. She feared nothing–neither the ambushes of men nor the dangers of the road. Nothing could trouble her, for she knew she carried within her a power that would overcome all obstacles.

On her way she composed her *Magnificat*. Supernatural strength upheld her. She could scarcely wait to tell Elizabeth of the great things that God had done for her. She wanted to sing with her who, as the Fathers of the Church say, personified the Old Law, the thanksgiving hymn of the New.

Joseph spent the three months of Mary's absence longing for her return. The days seemed endless, but immense hopes filled his soul. In only a little while he would welcome her into the home he had prepared for her–palatial as he could make it for his God-given queen. He did not know she carried within her womb a King, the Son of God Incarnate, he who would someday utter those awesome words: "If anyone wishes to come after me, let him deny himself, and take up his cross, and follow me...."

10

Joseph's agonizing passion

Joseph ... was minded to put her away privately
(Matt 1:19)

"And Mary," says the Evangelist "remained with her [cousin Elizabeth] about three months and return-ed to her own house" (Luke 1:56). These few words leave the home-coming to our imagination.

She came back happy at the thought of finding Joseph. But on the return journey she was not as light-hearted as when she had left home. She knew only a short time could pass before Joseph would know her condition, and the anxiety she felt could only be assuaged by singing a hymn of adoration, confidence and abandonment to the Divine Being whose temple she had become.

Nazareth. With what enthusiasm and over-flowing joy Joseph welcomed her. Happiness so over-whelmed him that at first he noticed nothing. Then, little by little, he began to see that his wife was pregnant. He could not doubt it. Outside the home, the news was received with joy. All the people of Nazareth came to congratulate the young couple.

A dramatic struggle then took place in Joseph's

soul. At first he tried to deny the evidence of his senses. He wanted to put a stop to the good wishes of the neighbours that were as sword thrusts in his heart. But soon he was forced to believe. He could not be mistaken. The signs were there, clear, brutal. Doubt was no longer possible. Mary carried a child in her womb. Face to face with this fact, his whole being was shattered; his soul fought for light in an abyss of total darkness.

Did he suspect Mary of sin? Certain Fathers of the Church–outstanding ones too–St Justin, St John Chrysostom, St Ambrose, St Augustine–think he did. The others–it is the opinion we adopt–find it impossible to think that for one instant St Joseph ever attributed to Mary anything unworthy of her. St Jerome's magnificent sentence covers the case: "Joseph knew Mary's holiness hid in silence a mystery he did not understand."

How could he have doubted her innocence? Think her capable of weakness? He repelled such a thought as criminal. He could more easily have believed someone who told him that the Jordan had returned to its source or the mountains of Hermon had vanished! She had remained just as simple, open, devoted, as before. She carried on her occupations quietly and straightforwardly as always. No shadow darkened her serene expression, belied her quiet smile. When she drew near him her eyes were as full of love and loyalty as they had ever been. She came to him for help, as always. No. There was no guilt here. Besides, he remembered her vow of virginity;

his own, for her sake.

But why did she not speak? Why this silence? Had he not the right to know the truth? With one word Mary could have turned his sorrow into joy. If she did not say that word it was because she had been told to keep the secret of the King. She felt –and rightly so–that the confidential message she had received should only be revealed by him who had sent it. She knew that God himself would make it known to Joseph in his own good time. Meanwhile she prayed and abandoned herself to Divine Wisdom.

This self-surrender did not keep her from suffering. Her silence called for heroism. Her heart was torn by Joseph's distress. She could sound the depths of his agony–and share it. On his ravaged countenance, thin and worn by anxiety and weariness, she read the sorrow she was unable to assuage. But still she kept silence. She guessed with what thoughts Joseph must be struggling. Had she not made a vow of virginity and told him of it? And now?

And indeed in Joseph's soul a frightful struggle was taking place. Never had God placed so holy a person, one so loved by him with a love of pre-dilection, in such a position. Night and day, hour after hour, he battled with his problem, tossed back and forth on the horns of this dilemma.

At first he had thought of questioning Mary. He tried in vain to speak. The words would not come. The questions stuck in his throat. Besides he was convinced that the silence of his betrothed veiled a mystery he was not worthy to share.

He found himself in the position of being able neither to keep Mary in his care nor expose her to the world. His loyalty forbade him to follow either course. He knew the iron ruling of the Mosaic Law which in such cases ordered an appeal to justice. Joseph was positive that Mary was innocent. He would find a way to set her free and at the same time safeguard her honour.

On his own side, should he keep her, he would be breaking the Law, since he had absolutely no rights over the child she carried, whose origin she hid from him. He had no part in this mystery; he could not build his marriage on a lie.

The Law prescribes how adultery is to be punished; the Bible text is clear. He could never allow Mary to be so treated. Precisely because he was a "just man", he could not bring her before the courts. He knew, all he knew, was that she was involved in a mystery he could not fathom, a mystery whose solution lay with God.

There was, then, only one thing for him to do, one risk to take. He would put her aside, not because he believed her guilty but because he reverenced in her a mystery. He must return her ring, take back the wedding gifts, and go away. No one would know where. He would be blamed for cowardly behaviour, for unfaithfulness–but no blame would fall on her.

He worked out his plan most carefully but put off its execution from day to day. Now, he could delay no longer. He felt that his sacrifice, a sacrifice more costly than that of Abraham's offering of his son Isaac, had been accepted by God. The final decision was made. He packed a few belongings. Before daybreak, he would go.

The words of the psalm were on his lips: "God, my God, why have you forsaken me? Why is this burden laid upon me?"

Joseph, because you were pleasing to God, temptation had to try you. Because in the thought of the Most High you were one day to be the hope of the despairing, the one to whom souls crushed by sorrow, plunged in darkness, could turn because you had passed through like temptations, endured a like agony. This trial was to prepare you for the role you were to fill in the future.

As you were to have the unique honour of being the adopted father of the Incarnate Son of God, you would first be marked with the Cross, the sign of man's redemption. The Cross would wound you where you were most vulnerable, in your love for her who after God held the first place in your thoughts and in your heart.

You were to take a principal part in the drama of our salvation; therefore you were to share in the sufferings it called for. You would not stand beside Mary when the Cross was raised on Golgotha, but beforehand you were to live through the mysteries of the Garden and Good Friday.

But to you too, Joseph, an angel will be sent to turn aside the sword, and God will be content with the holocaust you offer without waiting for its consummation.

11

The announcement made to Joseph

Joseph, do not be afraid... to take Mary as your wife
(Matt 1:20)

God had led Joseph to the very edge of the abyss of desolation; his cup of sorrow was full to the brim. The time for the inevitable, heartbreaking separation had come.

While waiting so that he might leave secretly, Joseph had stretched himself on his couch. God allowed sleep to overcome him, and suddenly as he slept an angel of the Lord appeared to him. It seems reasonable to suppose that it was the same angel who had announced to Mary that she was to conceive the Saviour–Gabriel, to whom had been confided all the events connected with the mystery of the Incarnation.

While Joseph thought about these things, St Matthew tells us, "an angel of the Lord appeared to him in a dream, and said, 'Joseph, son of David, do not be afraid... to take Mary as your wife, for the child conceived in her is of the Holy Spirit. She will bear a son, and you are to name him Jesus; for he will save his people from their sins' " (Matt. 1:20-21).

It would seem from this text that Joseph's sleep had been often broken by nightmares, and that even in sleep his unhappy thoughts continued to torment him.

"Joseph, son of David," said the angel. The poor village carpenter, conscious only of his littleness, is addressed with respect, hailed as the descendant of kings. He is given his title of nobility, for now the time has come for him to become that royal soul in whom the promises once made to his ancestor David are to be accomplished.

"Do not be afraid... to take Mary as your wife." If Joseph were getting ready to leave Mary, it was not because he doubted her but because he feared that in staying with her a fatherhood which he dared not assume would be attributed to him, a fatherhood in whose mystery he dared not intrude, lest in doing so he offend his Lord.

"For the child conceived in her is of the Holy Spirit." This sentence solves the enigma, reveals the unspeakable grandeur of that which has been accomplished in the womb of Mary. It is a conception which is the work of the Holy Spirit himself. The Eternal has entered there where neither flesh nor blood could have a place.

"She will bear a son, and you are to name him Jesus; for he will save his people from their sins." Though Joseph has no part in his conception, he is not to consider himself a stranger to this child. On the contrary, he is to exercise the rights and duties of a real father toward him, and to begin with he is to give him his name, Jesus. That name will signify what that mission is to be, for Jesus means Saviour. He has come on earth to deliver men from the worst kind of slavery– sin. To do so is to affirm his divine origin, for who but God can deliver mankind from sin?

Joseph did not converse with the angel as had Mary on the day of her Annunciation. He asked no questions. He received God's message; he understood perfectly. He had no need for further enlightenment. It was enough that his fears had been dispelled and his help asked. He may be likened ahead of time to the centurion mentioned in the Gospel whom Jesus told what to do and he did it.

It was while he slept the vision came. It was certainly a prophetic vision which left no room for doubt or illusion, but brought with it the certitude that the message was straight from God. Joseph knows he did not dream it. What he heard God had made him hear, by means of an angel.

He awoke, his whole being alive with joy. His happiness outweighed his former agony. All shadows fled away. The storm was stilled. The iron chains that bound his heart were loosed. Free, free at last he rejoiced, he exulted, his heart bounded with joy. His eyes were opened, all was glory, all was light. He realized that God had put in his care not only what was the most precious treasure on earth but, as Monsignor Guy says, "that which surpasses in worth all possible universes."

He understood that the child who had taken flesh in the womb of his affianced wife was the Messiah for whose coming he had so fervently prayed. He recalled the text from Isaias: "A virgin shall conceive, and bear a son." Mary is that virgin foretold in the prophecy. This does not surprise him. He knows her virtue, her holiness; he knows she is worthy to be the tabernacle of the Most High.

At the same time the role he is to play opens before his eyes. He understands that Mary is far from ceasing to be his wife in becoming the mother of the Son of God, and that he should not think of himself as an intruder in this family but rather as one chosen by God to safeguard her honour and that of her infant. Their official marriage, their loving devotedness to each other will provide the greatest possible protection. Without him, the mystery of the Incarnation could not have been made manifest under circumstances so happy and secure.

He realized fully the seriousness of his office. It placed on his shoulders a burden at once the most exalted and most overwhelming that a human being could bear.

He asked himself how he, a simple village workman, could ever have been chosen for this role. Far from being puffed up, he was penetrated through and through with the conviction of his lowliness and poverty. He told himself, however, that such was God's will, and this thought put an end to all his fears and hesitations. Certain of God's help, he felt able to bear the weight of his responsibility.

At once he gave his consent. It would not be like him to answer heaven's favours by protesting his inability, his unworthiness. When the Almighty speaks, the thing to do is to answer yes at once.

So the Gospel tells us, "Joseph, arising from sleep, did as the angel of the Lord had commanded him" (Matt 1:24). It is easy to imagine what that exact statement meant. Quickly he undid the bundle he had prepared for his flight, and at daybreak he hurried to Mary's house. When she opened the door, she did not need to be told what had happened. His glowing countenance, his radiant smile revealed that God had made known to him the mystery. At once he told her of the angel's visit and the order given. And Mary for the first time poured into human ears an account of what had taken place when the Incarnation of the Word was announced to her.

Then with still greater love and tender respect, Joseph gazed at her in wonder. He found her more beautiful, more holy than before because of what God had wrought in her, the flower of Jesse, who bore the seed foretold by the Prophets and longed for through the ages.

Then, using the words which Mary had told him she had heard from the angel and from Elizabeth, he addressed her with that salutation which will be repeated till the end of time: "Hail, Mary, full of grace; the Lord is with you: blessed are you among women, and blessed is the fruit of your womb, Jesus."

And in her turn Mary again sang her *Magnificat*. They then spoke of their final wedding ceremony, both of one mind in thinking it should be soon.

Custom called for it doubtless, but Joseph thought more of obeying the orders he had received from heaven and of proving how anxious he was to enter wholeheartedly into that mystery in which it was God's will he should share. She did belong to him already, it is true, but, when he had said his *Fiat* at the espousal ceremony, he had intended to enter into an alliance with a simple Palestinian virgin. But here was the Virgin-Mother of the Messiah, and it was God who commanded him to take her now after the miraculous change to his home.

He was in haste to pronounce that second *Fiat* which would unite them indissolubly and completely in a future destiny, filled with sorrow perhaps, but which he would share with the Co-Redemptrix of the human race.

12

The husband of Mary

*And Jacob begot Joseph, the husband of Mary, and
of her was born Jesus who is called Christ*
(Matt 1:16)

The gospel of St Matthew states that after the
apparition of the angel, Joseph did as he had been
told and took Mary to his home. This seems to show
that customs of the time did not give him the right to
have her live with him before the final contract.
Hence his hurry to ratify the union already contracted
on the day of the espousals.

A very exact description of the nuptial ceremony
of the Jews of those days is available. Mary and
Joseph would of course obey every jot and tittle of
the Law, observe carefully every traditional rite.

Mary was dressed according to custom in a vari-
coloured tunic over which hung a very full mantle,
enveloping her completely. Under her veil, resting on
her carefully arranged hair, she wore a crown of flat
gilded disks.

As night fell, she was carried in a covered litter
to Joseph's home. The wedding guests, in white garments, each wearing a gold ring on his finger, formed
an escort around the palanquin. A group of young

girls holding lighted lamps walked in front, while on either side others waved myrtle branches above her. All the people in Nazareth, on hearing the music of flutes and tambourines, gathered on the road to congratulate the bride. How little they dreamed that the chosen one of God was passing by, carrying within her their long-desired, long-awaited Messiah.

At the threshold of his home, Joseph was waiting. He wore a long white robe and he was crowned with a headpiece made of gold brocade.

When they met, the bride and groom exchanged rings and then seated themselves facing Jerusalem. Mary was on Joseph's right on the raised dais under a tentlike covering richly decorated and covered with gold ornaments. Again the contract was read, the same that had sealed their first vows. They were given to drink from the same cup which was then broken at their feet. These gestures signified that they must be ready henceforward to share their sorrows and joys.

Then a banquet was held, probably at the inn in Nazareth, and, in an atmosphere of joyful celebration, the feast lasted for several days, according to custom.

At last Mary and Joseph belonged to one another. They were united before God and man. God had reserved Mary for himself, but it pleased him to leave his chosen one, blessed among women, to be cared for by an earthly protector. In Joseph's hands he placed her whom he had so lovingly created, of whom from all eternity he had thought, of whom he was jealous with the jealousy of God.

Nothing was ill-assorted, however, in this

marriage. All was as it should be. Mary, called to be the Mother of God, filled with every grace fitting for this high vocation was holier than Joseph it is true, but Joseph had heard the angel's words assuring him that all was well: "Joseph, do not be afraid... to take Mary as your wife."

An added meaning to those words might be inserted here: "Take courage. You are indeed the one chosen to be the husband of her who has conceived by the Holy Spirit. You are equal to the task. To be the spouse of the Mother of God is a crushing burden for a human creature, but what is impossible to man is possible to God. All the necessary graces will be yours."

There is nothing unreal about the marriage of Mary and Joseph. Never, in fact, had earth seen a more perfect union, a love so deep, so glorious. For they loved each other in God.

The Holy Spirit hovered over their loving union, drawing them ever closer into the tender embrace of the Thrice Holy God. He was the foundation of their being. In adoring him, their souls were joined. He was the seal of their oneness.

It was this that made the strength and beauty of their marriage. In his Epistle to the Romans, St Paul writes: "For I am sure that neither death, nor life, nor angels, nor principalities, nor things present, nor things to come, nor powers, nor height, nor depth, nor any other creature will be able to separate us from the love of God, which is in Christ Jesus our Lord" (Rom 8:38-39).

That was the secret time-beat which every instant throbbed in the hearts of Mary and Joseph. As divine love is incorruptible, so their love springing from it was invincible, and indeed, far from distracting them from God, it helped to unite them closer to him. It was so from the time of their first vows. Joseph then thought he could never love Mary more than at that moment, but after the angel's revelation she became dearer still. The strength of his attachment made him a new man. The Infant-God that she carried increased his reverence, since he looked upon her as a new Ark of the Covenant and a Tabernacle of the Holy of Holies.

As for Mary, she saw in Joseph the representative of Divine Authority, the one chosen to be God's coadjutor in the mystery of the Incarnation, and always she showed him deference, submission and tender affection. Their vows of virginity served but to unite them more closely. It was because their love had in it no fleshly desires that it was untroubled by anxiety, doubt, bitterness or disappointment. Virginal love is without spot or wrinkle. They knew nothing of what St Paul calls the "tribulation of the flesh" (1 Cor 7:28). Holy in mind and body, their affection for each other was capable of constant enrichment and increase: "O holy virginity," cried Bossuet, "your fires are stronger because they are free; the flames that burn in us can never equal the ardour of the chaste embrace of souls whom love of purity binds together."

It would be a great mistake, however, to imagine that their spiritual attachment had in it nothing of the senses. There is no reason to think that they were deprived of that tender natural attraction deep in the heart of those who love.

Joseph perhaps had the presentiment that Mary, because of her mission, would one day be named by the whole world "cause of our joy". In any case, now living with him in his home, where until death they would be together, she was and could be the constant cause of his joy.

And Mary? She treasured in her heart all Joseph's words and acts of delicate thoughtfulness, and she gave him in return the joyous and devoted service of a loyal wife, foreseeing each desire, granting every wish. Their great delight was to see how best each could please the other. "I am a little servant," said Mary. "No, God himself appointed me to serve you." And so it went.

And now while Mary spun and hemmed swaddling clothes, Joseph fashioned the cradle wherein very soon the Son of the Most High, the King of Creation, the Saviour of the world would lay his infant head.

13

Bethlehem

*And Joseph went... into Judea to the town of David,
which is called Bethlehem* (Luke 2:4)

It is impossible to imagine without deep emotion
the intimacy in which Mary and Joseph spent the final
months before the infant's birth. Did they search the
Scriptures, study the prophecies concerning the coming of the Messiah? If so, it was not with vain curiosity but in order to prepare themselves more perfectly
for the event so close at hand. In those texts that
seemed especially to point to the Messiah, they would
insert the name Jesus.

One such text, from the Prophet Micheas which
mentioned Bethlehem as the place of his birth, filled
them with surprise and trepidation:

But you, O Bethlehem Ephrathah, who are little
to be among the clans of Juda, from you shall come
forth for me one who is to be ruler in Israel, whose
origin is from of old, from ancient days (Mic 5:2).

Micheas certainly had not made a mistake, but
how did it happen that he mentioned Bethlehem
instead of Nazareth?

Then one morning the town crier announced that
the Emperor Augustus had decided to make a census

of his subjects. Because the organization of the Jewish state divided the citizens into families, tribes and races, all were to remain in or return to their ancestral homes to be registered by the civil authorities.

To many, this Augustan edict caused much trouble and vexation. "Does this emperor want to count the children of Israel as if they were so many beasts?" There were certainly many angry protests and much indignation.

As to Mary and Joseph, far from finding fault with that authority to which it was God's will they should submit, their hearts beat high when they heard the proclamation. Their ancestral home was Bethlehem, as they were of David's line. Bethlehem, the little town of which they had read in the prophecy of Micheas! The decree was providential. They would go to Bethlehem to register. For Mary would go too, either because she was her parents' heiress or because women between the ages of twelve and sixty were bound by the civil law.

Husband and wife prepared for the journey and started off. Joseph's carpentry work made it necessary for him to own an ass. Mary would ride the ass and Joseph would walk beside her, staff in hand and loaded with their baggage. So artists through the ages have pictured the little family.

Five days would have been needed to cover the distance–about one hundred miles–from Nazareth to Bethlehem. They travelled by the caravan route passing through Jerusalem, Bethel, Bethulia. It was the winter season. The roads were bad. Even though

Mary, because of her miraculous motherhood, may have been spared much that would ordinarily have resulted from her condition, there was much suffering, many inconveniences.

In Jerusalem they would have prolonged their overnight stay by a visit to the Temple. There the singers in plaintive chant voiced their deathless longing: "When, O Lord, will you send the Saviour you have promised?" Husband and wife must have wanted to cry out "He is here; your Saviour is close to you. Hidden still, but in Bethlehem, as it is written, he will be made known!"

On the last day of the journey, the travellers saw Bethlehem nestled in the mothering hills, the pink houses surrounded by vineyards and gardens which had won for the little town the name, "Ephrata", flowering and fruitful, and their hearts thrilled with joy remembering that within those walls where David had lived, this Son of David would be born....

Keeping to the letter of the law of him who later would say, "Render, therefore, to Caesar the things that are Caesar's," they entered the village and registered at once as the census decree prescribed.

They stood in a queue with the others to be enrolled. Seeing her to be with child, did any offer Mary a prior place? In any case Joseph was there to protect her, if the need arose, from the impatient, crushing crowd.

They reached the census takers at last and presented themselves to the clerks who were closely guarded by soldiers in scarlet capes. The usual questions were asked. Joseph answered by giving the background of his family and present home: "Joseph, a carpenter in Nazareth, of the family of David.... His wife, Miriam, of the same family...."

Those who heard his words and saw the parchment he produced looked at them with some curiosity. How was it these descendants of kings were such ordinary simple people? The clerk, with complete indifference, registered them hurriedly as time was short, never surmising that because of this poor couple the whole world was being enrolled, in order that the prophecies concerning them might be fulfilled.

Joseph took his oath of loyalty and paid the tribute money. Now he set out to find a suitable lodging for Mary. It was not easy. The village was filled with strangers who like themselves had come for the enrolment, and he began to get uneasy. Elbowing his way through the crowd of men, donkeys and conveyances, he went first to the inn. He asked the innkeeper if he would put them up for the night–his wife and he. For himself any small corner would do, but at any moment his wife was expecting the birth of her child and she would need privacy and quiet.

The innkeeper looked the modest couple up and down. Obviously they were poor and could afford to pay very little. He told Joseph he was sorry but the house was crowded from cellar to roof. There was no room in the inn.

Joseph's heart was heavy. With Mary he threaded his way down the village street, knocking at door after door. Everywhere the answer was the same. The house was crowded; there was no room. Far from showing pity for Mary, no householder, in spite of Joseph's pleas, wanted to be embarrassed by a child-birth taking place in his home, especially when every home was so overcrowded.

In a celebrated painting, Luc Olivier Merson has pictured the scene. It is night. Joseph is standing before a closed door on which he has been knocking. A window is opened and a face appears. A voice orders him to go away–at once, at once. In another part of the picture, Mary, having heard the harsh words, is kneeling in the road, asking the unborn child to forgive those who refuse to receive him.

Mary and Joseph feel no bitterness nor do they complain. They not only do not blame those who refuse them help, they are sorry for having impor-tuned them.

Finally someone tells them where they can find a kind of shelter. There is a cave–innumerable caverns were to be found in the chalk hills of Judea–where animals are often housed and which has served now and again as a refuge for wanderers. Driven by extremity, they go to find the cave.

It was indeed a miserable lodging, dark, airless, reeking of smoke and animal smells. The floor was littered with refuse and old straw. Cribs for fodder ran the length of one wall. Tradition tells us that they found an ox and an ass tethered in the stalls.

Poor Joseph. The rebuffs he had received lay heavy on his heart. "Bethlehem," says Faber, "was his Cross." He blamed himself for the disappointments and refusals they had met with. He accused himself to God and Mary for his lack of foresight. But Mary was unperturbed; she tried to comfort him, to console him.

She assured him that these humiliations were the mysterious workings of divine Providence. God, coming to save men from their sins, was from the beginning giving an example of complete detachment. She begged Joseph to pray with her, and they recited the verses of her *Magnificat*, that hymn of thanksgiving which would be always on their lips.

14

The starry night

They found Mary and Joseph, and the babe lying in the manger (Luke 2:16)

As soon as they had entered their wretched dwelling, Joseph set about putting the place in order as far as possible. He lit a stable lamp hanging from a hook in the rock wall; he swept the earthen floor and piled some straw in the corner to serve as a makeshift mattress for Mary.

When Mary told him she felt her hour approaching, Joseph quietly left the cave, knowing that as God alone had brought about her marvellous conception, God alone should be witness to this equally marvellous birth. He looked for some place not far away where he could stay. Sleep he could not; his heart beat too loudly in his breast.

Suddenly an inspiration warned him to return. He ran to the stable and pushed back the curtain he had hung at the opening. Even by the lantern's feeble light he could see, in the midst of the poor interior of the rock-hewn cavern, a glorious vision. The child was there.

Mary had made a manger of the straw and in it she laid the infant. She knelt beside the improvised cradle, her hands joined, her eyes fixed on him, in an ecstasy of love and adoration. Close at hand, heads bent, the two beasts seemed to wish to warm him with their breath.

Miraculously, without loss of her virginity, Mary had brought her child into our world. She had had no need to pay the price that other mothers pay. With her own hands she swathed the babe in the swaddling bands she had prepared.

It was night. The echo of prophecy came down through the ages: "The people that walked in darkness, have seen a great light: to them that dwelt in the region of the shadow of death, light is risen" (Is 9:2). The sun in that region had sunk to its lowest point; now it would begin its upward climb.

Hearing Joseph enter, Mary turned to him and smiled. She lifted the tiny form almost hidden in the crib and placed him in Joseph's arms.

This makes us recall another scene in the earthly paradise of Eden, when Eve gave to Adam the forbidden fruit, closing by that act the garden's gates to all her offspring. Now at Bethlehem, the second Eve gives to Joseph, and in him all men who will be saved, the blessed fruit of her womb.

Joseph was thus the first beneficiary of Jesus' birth. It would seem, too, that by this gesture of giving her child to him first of all, Mary points out Joseph as the one who should merit above all other saints our deepest veneration.

It is well to remember that ordinary infants at birth have little of the charm this one perhaps had. Or was this brother of all the redeemed just like the others? Did he make himself no exception to the general rule? We do not know. In any case, Joseph recognized here the Son of God, and he spoke to Mary of his beauty. Tears of joy filled his eyes as he pressed the child to his heart. Then fearing his unworthiness, sensing his awkwardness, he gave him back to his Mother. Then together lost in love, in prayer, in contemplation, they kept watch over the Son of God. They could not take their eyes away from this frail creature swathed in swaddling bands, who lay there murmuring contentedly. In most things like other new-born children, he outdid them in the poverty of his surroundings. In these he held first place.

Was it, could it be really true that here lay the ambassador sent by God, the royal Messiah of whose glory David had sung? 'The Lord said to me, "You are my son; this day I have begotten you. Ask of me and I will give you the nations for an inheritance and the ends of the earth for your possession" (Ps 2:7-8).'

*   *   *

At that period of history the whole Jewish world was looking for the coming of the Messiah, but no one expected him to come as a humble and unknown individual. At the moment Israel was under Roman domination. In their eyes, the liberator promised by God would assuredly avenge their national pride. He would come terrible and triumphant, powerful and rich. Winning for them wealth, might, prosperity, abundance, he would make Israel supreme over all nations.

Who then could have imagined a Messiah without crown or sceptre, palace or army, whose birth, like that of a beggar, would take place in a stable? "In such surroundings," says Bossuet, "as make it difficult to understand how Joseph could have believed in him."

But Joseph's faith, an impregnable bulwark, suffered no weakening, knew no change. Added to his former just, upright, pure life which had been a long preparation for the Messiah's coming, there was Mary, what she was, what she said. Illumined by supernatural light, he understood that these untoward circumstances hid unfathomable mysteries.

Not for a moment did he hesitate to adore this little prisoner bound by swaddling bands. Not for a moment did he doubt that this child, whom he saw only by the lantern's dim ray, was the liberator whose true dwelling was in light inaccessible.

As Mary had taught him in her *Magnificat*, he exalted the power of divine immensity hidden in human littleness. He heard in the inarticulate cries of this babe the eternal Today, the uncreated wisdom of the Word spoken by the Father.

His faith brushed aside appearances and unveiled divinity, while his lips repeated again and again the titles attributed to the child by the angel of the Annunciation: "Son of David ... Son of the Most High ... He whose kingdom shall never have an end ... Son of God ... Jesus-Saviour...."

This divine child, who for a palace and royal

robes was content with swaddling clothes and a stable, whose only aureole was made of the straw of his crib, had come from heaven precisely to teach men that true grandeur has no need of external trappings but is hidden under simple appearances, that true riches are found in spiritual detachment. If the homeowners of Bethlehem had found no room for him, it was because he wanted to come to us as love's beggar.

If he wept, it was because his tears would wash away the stains of sin.

St Joseph understood these mysteries in part at least, enough certainly to enter into them. He worshipped without words, in silence. Silence was his song of adoration. As he worshipped, the understanding of his mission widened and deepened. It was to him God had given his only Son to be cared for and protected. With what fervour he determined to carry out his task.

Looking at this child lying in a manger, whose guardian he was chosen to be, he was conscious of great peace, great strength flooding his whole being. He loved him as if he were his own child, flesh of his flesh–with a father's tender, protective love. He would be by love what by nature he was not. For him alone he would live.

Joseph renewed his promise to the heavenly Father, his promise to devote to this child each moment of his life, the strength of his arm, the sweat of his brow, the blood of his veins. He asked only the grace to be able to carry out his mission as God would have him carry it out.

15

The first drops of Blood

*And when eight days were fulfilled for his circumcision
... [Joseph] called his name Jesus*
(Luke 2:21; Matt. 1:25)

While Mary and Joseph continued lost in contemplation near the Word Incarnate lying in the
manger, an angel of the Lord appeared to some
shepherds watching over their sheep on a hillside not
far away.

"Do not be afraid, for behold, I bring you good
news of great joy... A Saviour has been born to you.
And this shall be a sign to you: you will find an infant
wrapped in swaddling clothes and lying in a manger."

The first invitation given by God to render
homage to his Son clothed in his human nature, was
addressed to the humble, the upright of heart, those
whom the Psalmist calls "the poor of Yahweh". They
were the privileged ones since they resembled the
ancestor of the Messiah, David, the Shepherd-King.
They were among those closest to him who some day
would say: "I am the good shepherd." These simple
men, leaving their flocks, went in haste to Bethlehem.
They were able to find the new-born child without
much trouble, since many in the little town could tell

them where to search. These people indeed knew the whereabouts of that young couple who had asked for shelter from them in vain. They had taken refuge in the stable-cave hollowed out of the rock. That's where, as the Gospel tells us, the shepherds found "Mary and Joseph, and the babe."

It was Joseph who bade these kindly rough men welcome. In a few words he told them how it was his family came to be in the stable. And then he led them to Mary. She, all radiant, fulfilling for the first time her office of Mother of God and Mediatrix, took her child in her arms and held him out to them. Joseph let the lantern rays shine on the infant's face that they might see him better. Instinctively these first worshippers fell on their knees.

So filled with emotion was Joseph's heart, so wonderful in its immense simplicity were the awe and reverence of these adorers, that to Joseph this visit of the shepherds seemed the coming of God himself. He accepted with gratitude the gifts they brought: milk, butter, honey, some lengths of wool, a new-born lamb perhaps. They promised to find a suitable place in the village where the little family could stay for a time.

When the shepherds, their souls alight with hope and joy, went back to their flocks, they told everyone they met on the way what they had seen and heard. Joseph too, as soon as it was possible, went out to inscribe the child's birth in the public register and then set out to find the dwelling of which the night visitors had told him. Tradition still points out the place to the traveller–"There," they say, "is where the

Holy Family stayed after they left the stable."

That may be so. What is certain is that Joseph had to look about for some way in which he could earn a living in Bethlehem. A hard-working man, he would have blushed to live on the charity of others. For the present at least they would have to stay in the village, since the rainy season had set in, and the child was too young to be taken on the long journey to Nazareth.

The Holy Family remained where they were till they left for Egypt, and it would seem that Joseph thought of making their permanent home in Bethlehem even after the exile. As the Scriptures called Bethlehem the City of David, chosen above all others, he might have thought it his duty and best for the Messiah to live there where he had been born and where he was known.

Eight days after a birth the Law required that a child be circumcised. Circumcision was a rite God prescribed to Abraham as a sign in the flesh of his eternal alliance with his chosen people.

Since this child was the Son of God, Joseph could have thought such a rite unnecessary; but he knew the time had not yet come for the Messiah to be revealed. As his miraculous birth had been hidden under the veil of marriage, it would be contrary to God's designs to make his identity known now. Consequently, the Law of Israel must be observed.

Friends, relatives, even those from a distance–including Zachary and Elizabeth–as was the custom, were invited for the ceremony. It was a joyful occasion, like baptism in our own times, and a family feast was held.

It was Joseph–and not a priest as many artists have supposed and so painted the scene–who had the honour of imprinting the traditional sign of God's People on the flesh of the Infant Christ. His words were, "Blessed be Yahweh, our God. He has sanctified his beloved from his mother's womb and engraved his Law in human flesh. He marks his sons with the sign of the covenant that they may receive the blessings of our father, Abraham." The assistants answered in the words of the Psalmist: "Happy is he whom you have chosen to be your son!"

As he made the incision, Joseph pronounced the name he and Mary had received from heaven. To Mary the angel of the Annunciation had said, "You shall call his name Jesus." And to Joseph also the message had come, "[Mary] shall bring forth a son, and you shall call his name Jesus." On this point God had conferred on Joseph a status equal to that of Mary, thereby affirming that he should exercise over the child the rights of a father, for in Israel the rite of circumcision was administered by the father.

It is quite probable that in carrying out this rite Joseph had not a clear and precise understanding of the symbolical value of his actions. He was satisfied in conforming himself to the Jewish Law, regretting at the same time the suffering he was causing the child. His own tender heart bled when he heard the cries of pain and saw the blood and tears flow.

We are the ones who must penetrate into the

hidden meanings of the rite performed by Joseph.

Among the Hebrews, the given name was of immense, of prime importance. Its signification depended usually on the circumstances surrounding the child's birth and prefigured his future. In this case, it was God himself who had chosen for his Son the name he was to bear, leaving to Joseph the glory of giving it to him. It was a name that pointed out with absolute exactness the Saviour's mission among men.

That name would one day be raised above the Cross on Calvary. That name, St Paul tells us, is above all names, at the sound of which every knee shall bow in heaven, on earth, and under the earth; that name which will be repeated with love in time and eternity.

The name Jesus was quite common in Israel. Others besides the son of Mary had borne it and would bear it. Specially applicable was it to Josue, the son of Nun, and to the sons of Josedech. But they were figures only of him who was to save not only from suffering or weariness or exile, but from sin and everlasting death. And not only one people but the whole human race.

In giving the name Jesus to the child, Joseph was holding the office of vicar for the Eternal Father. Conscious that the infant's destiny would verify the name– because it was engraved in his very flesh– Joseph was the first to address him by it. "Your name will be Jesus." In other words he could have said, "You will be the Saviour of the world. You are He on whom all the hopes of salvation contained in the Scriptures are based!"

And since Joseph was the minister of God who willed his Son to come to earth under the sign of suffering, the giving of the name was to be the beginning of that suffering which would go on and on.

Matching action to word, he inaugurated the mystery of the world's redemption. He caused the first drops to flow of that blood which in the hour of the Passion would pour forth as a river. He dug the source of that bloody stream of mercy and salvation which unceasingly will cleanse the world of sin. That tiny infant, who wept and struggled as he received his meaningful name, was beginning his mission as Saviour.

When the ceremony was over and the guests had gone, as Mary looked after the child's wound, from Joseph's lips fell time after time the syllables of that salvific name. What charm, what promise were in the name of Jesus. Long before St Bernard sang his hymn, calling it music to the ear, honey on the lips, joy in the heart, Joseph had tasted its sweetness.

Each time he pronounced the name Jesus, he recalled the mystery hidden in those two syllables. Like Mary at the Annunciation, he accepted in advance to undergo and share whatever trials and sufferings would result from the child's mission as Saviour, knowing already from past experience that all would redouble the sorrows of his fatherly heart.

16

Simeon's prophecy

*And his father and mother were marvelling at the
things spoken concerning him* (Luke 2:33)

It is surely not a coincidence that in all the pages
of the Gospel giving the account of Jesus' childhood,
Joseph, far from passing unnoticed, is always shown
as acting in concert with Mary. "Joseph went up to
Bethlehem with Mary ... While they were there ... The
shepherds found Mary and Joseph ... They carried
him to Jerusalem ... His father and his mother marvelled ... Simeon blessed them ... They returned to
Galilee ... His parents went every year to Jerusalem
... They found him in the Temple ... He was subject to
them ...."

Joseph filled the role appointed him by God, and
Mary did nothing without consulting him and submitting to his authority. It was he who was head of the
family. It is therefore to be expected that, forty days
after that wonderful night, he accompanied his wife to
Jerusalem, with the twofold object in view of her
purification and the presentation of the infant in the
Temple. Though certainly there was no need, since
her maternity only gave her virginity added glory,
Mary did not dispense herself from the Law. And he

who was himself God was in no way bound to submit to the general custom.

Mary and Joseph were of one mind, what the Law prescribed would be fulfilled to the last jot and tittle.

As they started out, their hearts sang because they were about to perform a religious act. They little dreamed that what they looked forward to with such joy would bring a tragic announcement of future sorrow.

The child, in Mary's arms and escorted by Joseph, entered for the first time that city which one day would drive Jesus, like Isaac carrying the wood for the sacrifice, outside its walls to Golgotha.

At the Temple gate, Joseph bought two young pigeons, the gift of the poor. As the bystanders probably noticed, this little family could not afford to give the price of a lamb.

Suddenly quite an unexpected event took place. Through the crowd of pilgrims, merchants and beggars, an old man, inspired by the Spirit of God, came forward. His name was Simeon, "a just man," says the Gospel, "who feared God." He was the living personification of Israel. His one longing was for the coming of the Messiah. When he saw Jesus in his mother's arms, warned secretly by the Holy Spirit dwelling within him that here was the Promised One, the Desired of the Nations, he drew near Mary and Joseph and asked to take the child in his arms. Then in a sort of ecstasy, blessing God, trembling with emotion, his eyes alight with love, he intoned a hymn of victory and thanksgiving:

O Lord, now you are dismissing your servant in peace, according to your word; for my eyes have seen your salvation, which you have prepared in the presence of all peoples: a light for revelation to the Gentiles, and for glory to your people Israel (Luke 2:29-32).

And the Gospel continues, "His father and mother were marvelling at the things spoken concerning him." Not indeed because the words just heard were a revelation, but because here was another inspired witness to announce to the world the Saviour's coming.

After having thanked God, Simeon turned to Joseph and Mary, blessing them in turn, encouraging them to carry out the task appointed them. Did he guess in so doing that all future generations would praise and honour them both as the holiest of God's people?

He blessed the two as one because both, though in a different measure, had been instrumental in bringing about the coming of the Messiah to this earth.

Then he addressed himself to Mary alone. He was not afraid to foretell to this young mother the terrifying events of the future: "behold, this child is destined for the fall and for the rise of many in Israel, and for a sign that shall be contradicted. And your own soul a sword shall pierce" (Luke 2:34-35).

In this prophecy and its fulfilment, Joseph was to have no share. Simeon seemed to wish to spare him the sorrowful knowledge of what would take place on Calvary, since he would not then be present.

But all the same, Joseph's heart was sword-pierced. He had understood the prophecy. How could he not grieve knowing the agonies his son and his spouse were one day to bear? And besides, the blow dealt him was the more cruel because the words– precise, exact– were nevertheless so vague he was left to imagine, to fear all kinds of torments.

Jesus was to suffer contradiction. What could it mean? Would he be rejected by the nation that had so long awaited his coming? Would men be divided into two opposing camps? The one blaspheming, the other falling on their knees? The one finding salvation? The other being lost?

Then the words concerning Mary were no less a torture. She too was to undergo measureless sufferings, all kinds of misfortunes!

How must Joseph have wished that all these could fall on him instead of on them. Let his own mission become a torment; he could bear it. But Mary– so sweet, so pure, so holy. Could it be possible that God had destined her for sufferings such as those?

It hurt him to have been spared by the old man whose words, nevertheless, had wounded him to the quick. Engraved in his soul, they saddened his life. He could no longer look at his child, his wife, without thinking of the unknown agonies they would have to undergo. Dreading for them the prophet's sword, he went his way with a wound in his heart that would not heal.

Strong and submissive, he never complained, never fretted. He who had given the infant the name

Jesus-Saviour knew instinctively that salvation is won only by suffering, and with a generous acceptance he pronounced his *Fiat*. He knew he longed to follow the Messiah and his mother on their path of sorrow, and he prayed: "Lord, though I am a man unworthy to collaborate in your redemptive designs, I ask that if you need a victim, here I am; take me, but spare them."

Joseph and Mary now entered the Temple. The simple ceremony was carried out without pomp. Joseph placed the two doves on the altar, wishing he could offer a richer gift. Over Mary, the priest recited the prescribed prayers.

From his girdle Joseph took out the five silver shekels to redeem him who was the world's Redeemer.

All was over. The priest finished quickly, little thinking he had taken part in one of the most momentous ceremonies ever held in the long and glorious history of the Temple. In the child he had looked at with such indifference he saw nothing that would reveal to him that here was the Word Incarnate who, coming into the world, had said to his Eternal Father: "I come, O God, to do your will."

The chosen family then prepared to go back to Bethlehem where Joseph had decided to make his home for the time being. The return journey was more subdued than that of their coming to Jerusalem. Simeon's words still echoed in their hearts. They spoke little. They had to get used to pain.

Mary, carrying the child in her arms, realized more fully the destiny that lay before him. With what love she held him close.

And Joseph. Deeper than ever was the understanding of his great, his awesome vocation: to serve, to nourish, to protect, till the fearsome day would come, the One who would be offered up as an oblation for mankind.

That evening, before going to rest, Joseph bent over the infant's crib, repeating and interpreting to himself Simeon's canticle: "Let not Your servant depart, O Lord, for the child You have confided to me has yet need of me till the time of his manifestation to the world, when he will reveal himself as the Salvation of all peoples and the light of all nations."

17

The journey into exile

Arise, and take the child and his mother,
and go into Egypt (Matt 2:13)

On the day of the Presentation in the Temple, Simeon had said of Jesus, "Behold, this child is set as a sign of contradiction." Joseph had not long to wait to prove how true were those words. Everyone in Israel had heard of Herod.

They knew of his life filled with scandals, cruelties, heinous crimes. He had murdered his wife and three of his sons. A Jewish delegation had gone to Caesar Augustus to say that the dead were better off than the living whom the tyrant persecuted. Joseph, however, was far from imagining that the man's anger and jealousy could ever be turned against Jesus. We do not know how much time elapsed between the coming of the Magi and the Presentation. The liturgy telescopes the feasts, leaving only a short while between each, but in reality there must have been a few months; some exegetes speak of a year or more.

The Gospels make no mention of Joseph at the time of the Magi's visit. Perhaps he had found employment at some distance from his home and was away at work when they arrived. Of course Mary, as soon as possible, would have sent him word of what was happening and he would have returned at once.

Having no right to unveil God's mysteries, he did not enlighten the Magi when they took him for the child's natural father. He must have been much intimidated in presence of this Oriental splendour, these noble lords and rich retainers. Unassuming and discreet, he effaced himself as much as possible, leaving to Mary the conduct of the visit. His heart, though, was filled with joy. He rejoiced that the wise and great, like the poor shepherds, had come from afar to honour Mary's son.

Joseph felt himself in union with the Wise Men. His faith was like theirs, open and strong, calm and courageous. One sign only, a star, had been enough to induce them to cross the desert. And on arriving at Jerusalem they had merely asked, "Where is he that is born king of the Jews?" They seemed neither repelled nor disappointed on having undertaken such a journey to find themselves at the end in the presence of a child of poverty who could not even speak. Far from showing surprise, with joy radiating from their countenances, they bowed before him.

As was customary among the Eastern peoples when visiting any superior, they came loaded with gifts. Beside the crib Joseph saw gold from Ophir, incense from Arabia, myrrh from Ethiopia: the gold to pay homage to the child's royalty, the incense to proclaim his divinity, the myrrh to honour his humanity.

At the sight of these symbolic gifts, Joseph renewed in his heart the offering he had made of his whole being. "I, too, my Jesus, acknowledge You as king: here is the gold of my love and service. I adore Your divinity: here is the incense of my faith. I proclaim You Saviour of the world: here is the protection of my arms and all my strength till death and after, to help You in Your work of salvation."

With Joseph, these were no empty words. The time was almost come to put them to the test. The Magi, having received a supernatural warning not to return to Herod, had gone to their country by another way.

Joseph too had had a serious warning. "An angel of the Lord," says St Matthew, "appeared in a dream to Joseph, and said, 'Rise, take the child and his mother, and flee into Egypt, and remain there until I tell you. For Herod will seek the child to destroy him.' So he arose, and took the child and his mother by night, and withdrew into Egypt."

Reading this Gospel text describing this important event in its customary serene style, one would think it quite a simple and ordinary occurrence. What faith, nevertheless, and what grandeur in the soul of Joseph these few lines reveal.

Far from being shocked by the command, he thinks only of carrying it out. Another person might have been completely nonplussed and upset. What! The Son of God forced to fly from men! The Scriptures say he would bring a reign of peace, and now almost at birth men are hounding him. He comes as Saviour to the world, and he cannot even save himself!

Joseph had heard the words, "You shall call his name Jesus for he will be a Saviour!" A strange kind of Saviour who must hide in the dark and flee into a strange country! What is his Father in heaven about? "Suddenly an angel appeared," writes Bossuet, "like a frightened messenger, almost as if the very heavens are alarmed and terror spreads there before coming to earth!"

He who wields the thunderbolts and has at his command legions of angels, has such a one less power than a miserable earthly kinglet, proud of his little troups! How strange it all sounds!

Furthermore Joseph might have complained that he was being driven about from pillar to post. He is not even given time to prepare for this flight into an unknown, unfriendly land. Only at the last minute is he warned in an offhand manner, "Stay there, till you get other orders!"

But where Joseph was concerned there was none of that. He had read in Isaias a text which he had made his own:

"For as the heavens are exalted above the earth, so are ... my thoughts above your thoughts" (Is 55:9).

Basing his faith also on Mary whose slightest suggestion brought quieting light to his mind, he did not take it upon himself to judge or criticize, much less condemn the adorable designs of God. Never did he complain of any anxiety he had connected with the child, either before or after his birth.

The order to escape from Herod by night was not more disconcerting than the fact of the Incarnation itself. It seemed to him a part of the same mystery.

After all, God could easily have done away with Herod and his plans had he so willed. All power was his. He moved the stars in the heavens, yet he came on earth to share our human lot. It followed he would be like us in everything. He had no need to perform miracles to escape persecution since his victory was to be over sin by means of humility and self-abasement.

Nor was he at this time to be martyred with the Holy Innocents, because his work had not yet begun.

Joseph was well aware that it was he, Joseph, whom God had chosen to serve Mary and the child, those two beings who were far dearer to him than life. If the angel was not to accompany them, it was because Joseph was to take the place of the guardian angel. And no one could be chosen to be the father of the Son of God unless he were willing to pay the price this sublime vocation called for. He too must take part in the work of redemption. Besides, he had but one desire, one passion, he longed for one thing only–to carry out the designs of God no matter what the cost.

He rose at once. He woke Mary and told her of the dream-command. Mary went to the cradle where in perfect peace–seemingly unconscious of the orders given concerning him–God, the Omniscient, slept.

Hurriedly, they made ready for their departure. In a bag of heavy sacking they packed the child's clothes, some coverings, some food. Joseph placed in his girdle what remained of the gold savings. He hesitated for a moment about taking his tools, but then fearing their weight might slow down their process he decided to leave them behind.

With the still sleeping child in her arms, Mary mounted the ass Joseph had brought to the door. At once they set out into the silent night. Choosing the most unfrequented roads, he led his two most precious treasures to safety.

18

The stay in Egypt

And Joseph remained there until the death of Herod
(Matt. 2:15)

In order to avoid passing through Jerusalem, the Magi had gone east to the Orient. Joseph took Mary and the infant by the westerly route to Egypt.

Many exegetes have wondered why Egypt was named by the angel to be the place of refuge. The mystical reasons they suggest are cogent, but the most obvious cause was that Egypt was the nearest foreign country– its frontiers could be reached in four or five days. Moreover, that country was looked upon as a usual place of refuge for those driven from Israel by persecution or famine.

In passing along that route Joseph may have thought of that other Joseph who eighteen centuries earlier, after being sold by his brothers into slavery, had travelled the same road all unknowing that in God's designs he prefigured the foster-father of the Messiah.

Joseph left all behind him–his home, his peace, his means of livelihood–not knowing what conditions he would find or how long his exile would last. As God said to Abraham, so to Joseph: "Leave your country, your family, your father's house and go to the land that I will show you." And he went at once to save Jesus and his mother from Herod's fury.

His heart torn with anxiety, he asked himself how they would be able to bear this inhuman exodus. Haste was necessary. Perils were many. He knew he must be ready to shield them from any danger that might threaten. He urged on the phlegmatic beast who stubbornly held to his usual slow pace as he carried the world's King wrapped in his mother's cloak.

Were we to believe the Apocrypha, countless miracles took place on the journey: troups of angels guarded them; animal and plant life combined to feed and shelter them....

The reality was quite different. Had Jesus not had Joseph to watch over him, he could not have been more destitute, more abandoned, more exposed to danger.

Several nights had to be spent in the open. In the daytime the scattered nomad villages had to be avoided. They often looked back to see if they were being followed. Often they had to guess which road crossing to take. Travellers they met looked questioningly at them, evidently wondering why these three poor creatures were wandering in this forbidding desert, and where they were going with none to protect them.

Meanwhile, Herod's bloody order for the massacre of the children in Bethlehem was being carried out.

But the little family hurried on. They stopped only for Mary to nurse the child, or when they came to a spring that they might drink and refill their water-bag.

Exhausted, fagged out, their clothes threadbare, their feet cut and bleeding from the march, they reached the Egyptian frontier. Only then was their fear of Herod calmed. But there was another, that of entering a country which, after having driven out their ancestors, had become the centre of impious and idolatrous worship. Everything except the true God was adored: the sun, the crocodile, the ox.

The Apocrypha have it that when the Holy Family arrived in Egypt, the idols fell from their pedestals and were broken to bits. A tale with no foundation except the text from Isaias: "Behold the Lord ... will enter into Egypt, and the idols of Egypt shall be moved at his presence" (Is 19:1).

To reach the central cities six days more of travel were needed. They crossed the River Nile, remembering that Jacob's flocks had drunk its waters and the infant Moses had been found on its banks. The mighty pyramids loomed on the horizon, Cheops greatest of them all, whose building had taken the labour of 100,000 slaves for thirty years.

Painters have sometimes pictured our Lady with Jesus in her arms, asleep between the Sphinx's paws. Had anything like this been true, St Joseph, before lying down on the sands, rolled in his blanket, might have thought that the riddle which had puzzled the world from the time of the earthly paradise had its answer in the sleeping child and his mother.

If we accept tradition, the Holy Family lived some time at Heliopolis where there was an important Jewish colony. It was there that Ptolemy Philometor had permitted the construction of a temple rivalling in richness and splendour, if not in the veneration paid it, that of Jerusalem itself.

The same traditions tell us of several other places to which Joseph moved his family, probably in his effort to find work. When anyone is poor, a stranger, ignorant of the language, having no tools and, what is worse, not being able to give satisfactory reasons and motives for having left one's own country, it is not easy to make a living. There are the suspicious looks, the insolent smiles, the whispers....

The one-time scene at Bethlehem is repeated. He knocks on door after door. Timidly he asks if there is carpentry work of any kind needed. With the same courage as before, he bears every rebuff: "I would gladly go hungry, but do not, O Lord, let my wife want for bread!" Such was his prayer.

Suggestions were offered, of course. He must have got accustomed to enforced idleness, to long hours spent in the yards or the market place to which contractors came to hire a man for a day, whom they would pay the minimum wage for backbreaking labour. Though not used to such work, sometimes he was forced to take it.

But when Joseph came back in the evenings to Mary, her tender sympathy, the smiles of the Infant Jesus when he held him in his arms were consolation and recompense enough.

It is reasonable to imagine that Mary, too, skilled as she was in weaving and embroidering, found means to help her husband. We can see her also, hurrying through the streets to deliver the finished work, or seeking more, like any poor seamstress of our day.

Their lodgings also must have been very undesirable, obliged as they were to move from place to place. There were not always Jewish settlements where they could be given wise directives and alms. At times Joseph might have collected wood or wattles with which to build a lean-to shack against a ruined wall. At times they must have been content to find shelter under some steps or in an archway, sharing it perhaps with those whom today we would call tramps.

What is certain is that in Egypt they experienced isolation, loneliness and all the ills that followed from the circumstances in which they found themselves.

Most likely the inhabitants took them for Galilean workers who had come to Egypt under the false impression of being able to better themselves. They shrugged their shoulders at such guilelessness.

But the little family did not reveal the true cause of their exile. As an extra precaution they took care not even to pronounce the name of their ancestral village. In no way did they regret being in need. Jesus at his birth had given them an example. They knew it was of his free choice he had been born in a neglected stable. They found comfort in remembering that the life of poverty and privation he shared with them was according to his will, and they in turn were happy to prolong for themselves the mystery of Bethlehem.

19

The return to Nazareth

*So he arose and took the child and his mother, and
went into the land of Israel* (Matt 2:21)

St Matthew's gospel has only a few words to
tell of the sojourn of the Holy Family in Egypt. "...
[he] remained there until the death of Herod; that
what was spoken by the Lord through the prophet
might be fulfilled, *Out of Egypt I have called my
son.*" A laconic statement–nothing more.

How long did their stay last? The answer can be
based only on conjecture, and there are countless
opinions on the subject. St Bonaventure goes so far
as to suggest seven years; some Fathers of the
Church, a few months only. The Apocryphal writers,
in order to allow sufficient time for all their miracles
to have taken place, allow three years for the exile.
But exegetes advance weighty reasons for limiting the
time to one or two years.[19]

---

[19] R. P. Durand, S.J. (The Gospel of St Matthew) writes: "Herod died in the spring of
the year 750 of Rome, seven days before the feast of Easter. On the other hand, as the
date of the Nativity of Jesus Christ cannot be put back before 747, it follows that all the
events recounted by St Matthew and St Luke in their first two chapters, including the
stay in Egypt, must have lasted for a space of three or four years if it is supposed that
the Holy Family received the order to return immediately after the tyrant's death."

According to St Matthew: "But when Herod was dead, behold, an angel of the Lord appeared in a dream to Joseph in Egypt, saying, 'Arise, and take the child and his mother, and go into the land of Israel, for those who sought the child's life are dead.' So he arose and took the child and his mother, and went into the land of Israel" (Matt 2:19-21).

It is again through the instrumentality of an angel that God makes his will known to Joseph. "The services which this great man had to perform in secret in his dealings with the law-givers of the Blessed Trinity kept heavenly messengers continually on the run," writes St Leonard of Port-Maurice. It is the third time that the Evangelist tells of an angel's visit to St Joseph. And on the road going back to his country, for the fourth time the same angelic ambassador came to him.

One might wonder why it was during sleep that Joseph received these divine instructions, since others– Zachary and the shepherds of Bethlehem, for example –saw the angels while keeping their night watch. Moreover, the Church has always warned men against counting on dreams as a means of interpreting God's designs.

The usual answer is that, on awakening, Joseph was so convinced by grace that his dream was from God, so certain that these were the means chosen by God to make known to him his will, that he had absolutely no doubts on the subject. And if God did make use of this simple, unobtrusive manner of communication with Joseph, it was because he wished to emphasize for our sakes his strong living faith. The slightest sign, the most delicate touch were enough for this faithful servant, whose soul vibrated to the lightest breath of grace from God for the manifestation of whose will he stood in constant expectation.

This submission seems the more beautiful, the more sublime because he stands always on the watchtower, his lamp alight, waiting for his master's coming.

When Joseph got word that he could return to Palestine–there being no longer any danger–he was filled with joy. He looked at the child Jesus with a love all the greater because it had been threatened by the fear of losing him.

It was with heartbroken sorrow that Mary and Joseph had learned of the massacre of the Innocents. They had heard too of the horrible disease, the ulcer that had attacked Herod, the murderer of the infants; of the unpleasant evidence of illness that filled the palace. Worms infested his body long before death. He had tried to kill himself but had been prevented from doing so. It seemed as if willy-nilly he was condemned to endure here on earth the punishment for his crimes. His last inhuman act was a command that his son, Antipater, be executed.

Joseph's happiness at the thought of his homegoing was not unmixed with anxiety. He wondered, since the angel had said nothing on the subject, to which city he should return, whether or not he would find his home and workshop in good condition, what he should answer when people questioned him as to his absence and the reason he had left.

Desirous as always to do God's will, he hurried forward the preparations for his departure. He was leaving Egypt where he had suffered more from the atmosphere of idolatrous worship than from the actual privations he had been obliged to impose on his little family.

Tradition tells us that on their return journey they took the route along the coast. It was the shorter and easier way. They might even have boarded a ship in one of the Egyptian harbours, such as Alexandria. So, anyhow, runs the Coptic legend.

On the four- or five-day trip, Joseph, conscious of the responsibilities placed upon him, listened to the conversations of his fellow travellers and asked them about the conditions in his own country. The ship disembarked her passengers at Ascalon or Joppa. Joseph had at first intended to settle in Bethlehem, thinking, because of the prophecies, that such was the will of God. Perhaps, too, he counted on finding work there more easily than at Nazareth, since, as is the case even today, employers go to Bethlehem to seek out seasonal workers.

He had not yet fully made up his mind on reaching the frontier; there he learned that Archelaus was reigning in Judea. The news made him fearful about entering that province. Archelaus was proving like his father. He had just had three thousand of his subjects strangled in the Temple precincts.

Joseph thought Galilee would be a safer haven. It had been allotted to Herod Antipas, who seemed at the time determined to govern with justice and benevolence. Once again a dream came to confirm Joseph's choice. Though Micheas' prophecy had put Bethlehem among the chosen cities, another oracle had also named Nazareth.

So as not to add to Mary's weariness by further hurried travel, such as had been forced on them till then, they now journeyed more slowly and in shorter stages. On their arrival at Nazareth the little family was warmly received by friends and relatives who, of course, wanted to know all about them–why they had left Bethlehem so abruptly, where they had been, and so forth. They answered as best they could without giving anything away or equivocating.

Their former house was rather dilapidated and in need of repair. They spent no time in condemning those who had helped themselves to their belongings during their absence; after all the place had looked as if it were abandoned by its owners so no one could be blamed for pillaging it a bit.

At once Joseph began to put things in order. He filled the cracks in the walls, he whitewashed the outside. He set about looking for his old customers. Little by little the shop was fitted up again with tools, the yard stacked with planks. Above the door he hung a large sign to show he was again ready for work: Joseph–Carpenter.

20

They found him in the Temple

*When they were returning, the boy Jesus remained
in Jerusalem, and his parents did not know it*
(Luke 2:43)

The Law required that all Israelites go on
pilgrimage to the Temple in Jerusalem on each of the
three great feasts of the year: the celebration of the
Pasch, of Pentecost, of Tabernacles.

If they lived at a distance–as was the case of
those in Nazareth–it sufficed to come for one of these
feasts only. Women were not bound by these pre-
scriptions, but it was the custom nevertheless for them
to accompany their husbands. It is obvious that Joseph
and Mary would omit no jot nor tittle of the Law.

Now when Jesus reached his twelfth year, he
became at the same time "a son of the Law" and was
bound to observe it. He went up to Jerusalem with his
parents. We see them as part of the caravan, singing
the songs customary on the occasion: "The canticle of
those who ascend," and the Psalm, "As the hind longs
for the running waters, so my soul longs for you, O
God." There were other quotations from the Psalms:
"Those who trust in the Lord are firm as the found-
ations of Sion"; "How good and how pleasant it is for

brethren to dwell together in unity!'"

The Holy Family remained in Jerusalem a full week: Mary, whom we hail as Mother of the Universal Church; Joseph, the future Protector of the same Church; Jesus, eternal God, the head of the Church. They were now lost in the crowd, not seeking to make themselves known, claiming no special privileges, jostled and pushed about, accepting the least desirable places in the Temple from where to assist at the ceremonies of religious worship.

When the feast days had ended, the members of the caravans assembled in the places appointed. There was all the wild, noisy excitement customary among Orientals till things finally settled down and the return journey was begun.

The members of the caravans were to meet in the evening after a full day's travel. When Mary and Joseph joined each other, they were horrified to find that Jesus was missing. It was not astonishing that they had not been aware of his absence before this late hour. As he was now twelve years old and "a son of the Law", a certain amount of liberty to go where he wished was granted him. His parents would have been considered too officious had they tried to keep him under their wing. He had been free to join the company of men or to go with the group of women. Joseph, not seeing him in his own party, thought he was with Mary and rejoiced that it would be so. Mary, on her side, was quite certain he was with Joseph, and knew what joy his presence would give his father. Perhaps Jesus had told his mother before the caravan started that he would stay with his "Father," and Mary had not realized which "father" he was speaking of.

In any case their hearts were heavy with sorrow and anxiety. A thousand contingencies presented themselves to their minds. Was he lost? Had evildoers got possession of him? Or had he perhaps left them on his own account to carry out his mysterious mission? Had the hour come when the sword prophesied by Simeon was to pierce the mother's soul?

Around them, perhaps, people were making disparaging remarks: "Had they looked after the boy more carefully, they would not have lost him...."

They turned back to Jerusalem at once, following the road by which they had come. They walked in silence, their souls weighed down with sorrow. Joseph's pain was as great as Mary's. In the earthly paradise Adam had blamed God, and Eve had blamed the serpent. Here, each one took the blame and excused the other. Neither wished to humble or make the other responsible for the trial that overwhelmed both.

Joseph asked himself if God were punishing him for failing in his mission. He told Mary it was so. "No, no," she answered, "it was my duty to watch over him."

On reaching Jerusalem they searched the highways and byways. For three days they walked the streets, the lanes. It was a sort of preview of the way of the Cross when their son would carry the True Cross on his shoulders.

They questioned all whom they met. They described the boy. But no one had seen him. No one knew anything about him. If in the distance they saw a child about his height, they hurried to overtake him. One more disappointment.

At last, on the third day they found him. He was seated in one of the vast halls of the Temple, in the midst of the Doctors who, according to the Jewish custom at the Paschal Feast, organized a theological congress where great learning was displayed and many subjects discussed with subtle argument. He sat like a schoolboy in the presence of the Elders who on questioning him were amazed at his wisdom and his answers.

Seeing him, Mary and Joseph could not hide their surprise. It was the first time Jesus had allowed a ray of his uncreated knowledge to appear. But how could he, who until now had given evidence of possessing every filial virtue, how could he have withdrawn from their authority and so calmly have allowed his parents to undergo such cruel suffering? How could he have done this to them?

They knew they must speak, but Joseph felt Mary had the greater right to intervene in these circumstances as she had a greater share in the mystery of the Incarnation.

From her lips escapes a cry that reveals to its depths her mother's soul: "Son, why have you treated us so? Behold, your father and I have been looking for you anxiously." A loving, tender reproach. The desire, too, to know the reason of this action so foreign to the thoughtful, habitual respect hitherto shown them.

Jesus makes no attempt either to excuse himself or ask their pardon, but in answer to the question his mother has the right to ask, he replies: "How is it that you sought me? Did you not know that I must be about my Father's business?"

Jesus' answer, made not with sternness but with a smile on his lips, could have had two meanings: He did not reproach them for having sought him, but why had they not come at once to the Temple, the one place where he would be because it was his Father's house? To hold to that interpretation alone would make us run the risk of losing the deeper and more sublime meaning.

Having ceased to be a child, Jesus would remind his parents of his divine sonship and his transcendent mission. He explained to them that the obedience he paid them was subordinate to that he owed his Father in heaven. They must realize that whatever should take place in his life was in absolute conformity to that divine will he had come on earth to do. As a result of this, many things will take place that will surprise them. He wishes to forestall their wonder, to prepare them for the "scandal" of the Redemption.

Before returning to Nazareth and enclosing himself in its silence and his former occupations which the Evangelist sums up in the words: "He was subject to them," he says to us, "Call no one on earth your father; you have only one father, he who is in heaven." He wishes to impress upon us that our principal occupation, like his own, should be to seek first and always the interests and glory of God.

His words do not signify that he wishes to throw off the yoke of submission to his parents–His love for them and his obedience to them are without a counterpart– but, as God has commanded men with solemn precepts to honour their parents, he would by his example show with what seriousness this commandment is to be put in practice. At the same time he warns us that our obedience must be hierarchical– first, the service of God and afterward all legitimate love and service.

The Evangelist tells us that neither Mary nor Joseph understood his words. Certainly they grasped their most obvious meaning, but they asked themselves why Jesus, who until then had never manifested the least sign of his divinity, had done so now in these singular and mysterious circumstances. What they certainly did not comprehend was that their child, still so young, completely breaking his habitual ties of obedience and submission, should at this moment so abruptly have declared himself the Son of God, throwing away, as apparently no longer endurable, the authority of his parents.

In their humility, they acknowledged that they could not fully grasp the meaning of his words. Indeed to have been able to do so would have meant that they were able to understand not only the mystery of the Incarnation but of the Trinity itself.

Joseph and Mary, like all created beings, were subject to the laws of progression. Jesus chose to rouse their religious curiosity, to place them on the road he would point out to those who would wish to become his disciples: "Ask, and it shall be given you; seek, and you shall find; knock, and it shall be opened to you."

21

Joseph's fatherhood

*Behold, your father and I have been looking
for you anxiously* (Luke 2:48)

St Luke seems to take a great deal of satisfaction
in giving Joseph the name of *father* and linking him
with Mary under the appellation common to both:
"*parentes ejus*", his parents.... This Evangelist, who
was Mary's confidant, knew better than anyone else
all that had to do with the birth of the Messiah and
that Joseph was not his father by carnal generation. It
must have been, says Suarez, by a special inspiration
from God that he employed this term.

We always find on Mary's lips the expression
used by St Luke. When she found Jesus in the Temple
she said, "Child, why have you treated us like this?
Behold, your father and I have been looking for you
anxiously." Also, in speaking of her husband she
gives him the title of "father". That is undoubtedly the
title they used in the privacy of their home in
Nazareth. But she, the Virgin most prudent, did not
hesitate to give him the same name in public before
the Doctors of the Law.

This was because, deeply enlightened on the
mystery of the Incarnation, she did not think it right to

conceal on this solemn occasion the truth that Joseph should in all sincerity be called the "father of Jesus".

It is important to look into this matter in order to understand what realities are hidden in this name.

In ordinary speech, two kinds of paternity are understood: the natural, which means the transmission of life and the resulting coming to birth of a new being; the other, paternity by adoption, a simple measure or proceeding by which a man declares he will accept and acknowledge legally as his own child one engendered by another.

However, neither of these cases applies absolutely to St Joseph. The first implies too much, the second, too little. It is historically and theologically certain that Joseph, according to the natural and ordinary mode of generation, was not the father of Jesus, who in his humanity was without a father.

Was Joseph only his adopted father, or his "putative" father according to the expression consecrated by usage and sanctioned by the liturgy in the Invitatory for the feast of March 19: "Let us adore Christ, the Son of God, who was willing on earth to pass for the son of Joseph"? It is the same term the Sovereign Pontiffs make use of in countless official documents.

Theologians are more inclined and more and more of one mind in declaring that the expressions putative (supposed) father, adoptive father, foster father are too limited in meaning and give but the partial truth. These titles, honourable as they are, express only a piecemeal, fictitious, borrowed paternity–a mere guardianship.

The reality far surpasses these qualifications. Adoption, for example, presupposes a stranger who chooses a child whom he treats as his own.

Now, at no time was Jesus a stranger to Joseph. From the moment he became incarnate in Mary, lawfully and divinely fruitful, he belonged at the same time to Joseph, since husband and wife, according to the order established by God are one, and hold their goods in common.

It is not easy to qualify Joseph's paternity with precision because it represents, if one may so express it, a paternity utterly unique in history; something so special, so original as to demand a new vocabulary capable of attributing a proper title to its function.

It must be remembered that the human generation of Jesus in the genealogy handed down by the Evangelist is that of Joseph. This fact should be emphasized. To use Bossuet's expression borrowed from St John Chrysostom: "God gave Joseph all that belongs to a father without loss of virginity." The meaning is that Joseph had no share in the natural conception of Jesus, but with that one exception his fatherhood embraced all the privileges, all the duties, all the rights of an ordinary father in his home, so that the title that best fits him is that of *virgin Father of Jesus*.[20]

---

[20] The Congress which was held from August 1-9, 1955, at the Oratory of St Joseph of Mount Royal in Canada, putting aside the more traditional formulas of "putative father", "foster father", did not hesitate to adopt the expression "virginal father" used in the prayer approved by St Piux X.

He was Jesus' father by reason of his marriage to Mary. Mary, because of the marriage contract formulated by law and sanctioned by God, was Joseph's possession. Consequently anything that would happen to accrue to Mary in the future, even miraculously, would become at the same time the property of Joseph, her husband. Moreover, Jesus having been born of the flesh of his wife, and that flesh Joseph's by reason of the sacred donation of gifts resulting from marriage, Joseph would have a necessary parental relationship with Mary in the fruit of her womb.

Over and beyond this, God made him indispensable in that intricate arrangement whereby the mystery of the Incarnation might be hidden in the bosom of a family bearing all the marks of an ordinary threefold relationship. The head of the home where the child was to be born could never be dethroned.

If all that has been mentioned implies but a negative role, the part of active agent played by Joseph in the birth of Christ must be affirmatively stated. The Man-God was the fruit of Mary's virginity. It was her purity so pleasing to God that drew down the Holy Spirit to accomplish his divine action within her. In a way, it was her virginity that made her fruitful. And Joseph, reverencing that virginity, prepared the way as it were for the Holy Spirit to make possible her miraculous fecundity. He respected that virginity, deemed essential by God. Both, by common consent, had offered it to heaven as an acceptable gift. And both in return had received in equal measure a son, the fruit as it were, of their virginal union.

Joseph did not, of course, give his blood to this son. But the blood of Jesus had to be nourished, sustained, enriched. And it was this humble carpenter who, by the sweat of his brow, was appointed to accomplish this task.

Jesus will eat the bread earned by Joseph's toil; in the strength of that bread he will grow to manhood; in the strength of that bread stretched on the Cross, he will save the world. It is by means of the food bought with the price of Joseph's toil that Jesus' veins will be filled with that Precious Blood which he will spill to the last drop on Calvary and which until the consummation of the world will be offered up on our altars in the Sacrifice of the Mass. Joseph then had an active share through the Blood of Jesus in the world's Redemption.

To call Jesus "his son", and to consider him so, was Joseph's right. The Fathers of the Church never hesitate to liken his presence near Jesus to "the shadow of God the Father". As Father Olier says, "He was like a sacrament of the Eternal Father beneath whose shadow God engendered his Word, incarnate in Mary."

And because the true Father of Jesus, he who begot him from all eternity according to his divine nature, entrusted to Joseph the task of being in some manner his vicar, he endowed him in some way with the infinite love he himself bore his son.

"You will give him the name, Jesus," the angel had said. In other words: "This child has no father but God. But to you, God transmits his own rights. You will be a father to him. You will have a truly fatherly love for him, and you will exercise all the rights of a father over him."

Joseph then loved Jesus as his son and adored him as his God. And the vision he had always before his eyes of a God loving the world with an infinite love became a stimulus for him to love his son always more and more and to serve him with ever greater generosity.

He loved Jesus then as if indeed he had fathered him. He loved him as a mysterious gift God had let fall into his poor human life. To him, wholeheartedly, unreservedly, totally, he consecrated his strength, his care, his time. His every thought was for him, and all without a wish for any reward save that of being able each day to make his consecration more perfect. His love was at once strong and gentle, peaceful and fervent, calm and intense, controlled and eager.

We can picture Joseph holding the child Jesus in his arms, rocking his cradle, singing him to sleep. He smiled lovingly upon him. He took him for walks, made toys for him. Like other fathers he played with his little son. The caresses with which he showered him were at one and the same time a proof of tender affection and a sign of adoring worship.

The Apocryphal writers take pleasure in making of the child Jesus a kind of prodigy, a worker of miracles, one who walked the earth wrapped in clouds of glory. None of this was true. The Man-God chose to live and to act as an ordinary child of his age would live and act. The Word of God spoke as other children spoke. In all things he was like them.

And Joseph, surrounding him with care and

tenderness, marvelled at seeing him sleep "who watched over Israel"; to see him weep "who was the joy of the elect"; to see the charming infant ways of him who was the creator of the universe.

According to Jewish customs, a male child in the family circle remained in the mother's care until he was five years of age; the father then began to assume an active part in his upbringing. He taught him the Law of God and the precepts of Moses.

What was Joseph's joy when the time came for him to take over these fatherly duties and to see his son "advance in wisdom and age and grace before God and men."

In his heart the words of the Canticle rose silently to God, telling of his joy, his gratitude:

'My Beloved is radiant and ruddy;

he stands out among thousands....

Sweetness itself, ... He is all delight.

My lover belongs to me and I to him' (Cant 5:10,16; 6:3).

22

The home in Nazareth

And he went down with them and came to Nazareth,
and was subject to them (Luke 2:51)

On finding Jesus in the Temple, Mary had cried out, "Child, why have you treated us like this?" She links Joseph with herself. And, as if she feared this child might not realize that she was not alone in loving and suffering for his sake, she emphasizes: "Behold, your father and I have been looking for you anxiously."

And in answering: "Did you not know that I must be about my Father's business?" Jesus does not disavow Joseph as "his father", but he raises their thoughts to his Eternal Father to whose interests all others must be subordinate. This was the first recorded occasion–and with what precision–on which he spoke of his Father in heaven.

Neither Mary nor Joseph asked anything further, even though they did not fully understand his meaning, but they kept all his words carefully in their hearts. For Joseph, too, gave himself up to silent reflection. He realized that for an instant, like a flash of lightning, the transcendence of this child had been revealed.

He felt, perhaps even more than Mary, the need to try to fathom the meaning of this answer; it seemed to minimize the status of the poor carpenter, in order to accentuate the claims of that other "Father".

He felt for a moment that he might have treated his son with too much familiarity. He realized how truly, how infinitely more Jesus belonged to his Father in heaven than to him. Yet the import of those words that underlined the distance between them was to be utterly reversed by the spectacle of his son's submission. The finding of Jesus in the Temple throws light on the mystery of Joseph as the marriage at Cana on the mystery of Mary.

Jesus' apparent refusal: "What is that to me and to you? My hour is not yet come ..." was to be followed by the first great miracle. It looked as if by his prior refusal to grant her request, he wished the more to glorify the triumphant outcome of her prayer. In the same way, the words that had seemed to Joseph to cast him aside as worthless served but to render the Evangelist's following statement the more wonderful: "He was subject to them."

Jesus began by showing himself master of those who were officially his teachers. He affirmed his divine sonship and consequently his sovereign independence, but only to make shine out more brilliantly the perfection of that obedience of which he gave us the example. He was to make it his endless duty to carry out perfectly whatever he was told to do. This was especially so in his obedience to Joseph, his father and the head of his family. His actions, his occupations, his meals, his sleep, all were as Joseph willed.

"The things that were his Father's." In submitting to his parents he gave glory to his Father. To his mother also, but to him who was "the shadow of the heavenly Father", whose authority was that of head of their little household, to him he submitted himself completely.

If Jesus' subjection showed his incomprehensible humility, it served also to emphasize the dignity of him whom he obeyed.

Jesus' words shone as a light in the mind of Joseph to show how best he could enter more deeply every day of his life into God's designs. The knowledge that between Jesus and himself there lay infinite mystery did not paralyze Joseph's thought or his action. On the contrary, it helped him to carry out straightforwardly his mission with regard to this child, his son in his humanity, his Lord in his divinity. His task was to reconcile these apparent opposites so as to command without constraint him whom he adored as God.

He was able, as a matter of fact, to do this quite simply, without fear or difficulty. It was the will of God–that sufficed. It was the will of God that he, Joseph, should exercise this authority. In doing so, then, he obeyed God.

If he had counted only on his faith, he might have cried out like St Peter, "You shall never wash my feet." But silencing his faith he accepted all the acts of service, of love and respect Jesus showered on him. On the other hand, Jesus' perfect example of obedience became for Joseph an inexhaustible source of humility.

God had appointed Joseph to educate the Word

Incarnate–a statement frightening but true. The hypostatic union joined the two natures in Jesus simply, perfectly, in such a way that, being God, he had from the first moment of his conception the fullness of wisdom and knowledge. But as man (and considered from a merely natural point of view), he was subject to the law of progress like other children who must be taught in order to learn, to whom everything must be explained.

Christ's life, his knowledge as God remained hidden from the eyes of men. His exterior actions were those of a child of his years. He had to be taught to walk, to speak, to read, to repeat word for word the famous texts of Scripture, to study nature and the marvels of creation. And that was the combined task of Mary and Joseph.

Joseph taught Jesus first of all by his example, by his bearing. In every child there is an innate tendency, an instinctive need to see in those around him what is to be done, and to imitate what they see. Mary's countenance and Joseph's were the first mirrors of perfection that Jesus looked upon. His father's gestures, conduct, manner of speech were the first actions after Mary's he observed. He looked upon him with reverence. Merely to see this religious man, this great contemplative was a lesson in itself.

"He was subject to them." He did nothing except in entire dependence upon them. He always showed them deference and respect. He foresaw their needs and with utter devotedness he hurried to serve them. His perfectly natural obedience was sometimes disconcerting. Never did any child pay more heed to a father's counsels, to the answers to the questions he asked. The honour he paid Joseph was religious, filial, since in him he saw the image of his Father in heaven.

Joseph taught him all things a father should teach his son. So deeply rooted in this boy were the human characteristics of Joseph that later on the title "Son of Man" could most fittingly be applied to him.

It was again Joseph who explained the Law, initiated him into the ritual, taught him the proverbs of his race, the history and traditions of his people. It was he who taught him to pray, since in Israel the obligation to do so belonged first of all to the father of the family. Over and over again he repeated with his son the great poems from the Bible:

> 'The Lord our God is the only Lord,
> You must love the Lord your God
> With all your heart, with all your soul,
> With all your strength....
> To God belongs your country;
> To God its destiny....
> It is the Lord our God
> Who brought us forth from the land of Egypt,
> That he might be in truth our God.'

And Jesus listened gravely to Joseph's words. Together with Joseph and with Mary–who being a woman would never, according to Jewish custom, have led the family prayer–each morning and each evening he chanted the profession of faith known to all faithful Israelites.

Attached to the framework of their door, as in all

other homes, a small box held the parchments on which certain texts from Scripture were written. When Joseph left the house, he made a gesture somewhat like that of a person nowadays about to take holy water. Were Jesus in his arms, he showed the child how to perform the same action.

It was Joseph, too, who early on the Sabbath took Jesus to the synagogue. They entered with heads covered, slippers on their feet. They listened to the readings from the Bible and the commentaries on the Law, and they made the customary prostrations in answering the litanies.

In the afternoons after having assisted again at the offices in the synagogue, they visited the sick, the old, the afflicted, the poor, all those of whom years later Jesus spoke on the mountain of the Beatitudes. Then also they took what was known as the "Sabbath Walk" which, as the Law required, had to be short.

With Mary and Jesus, Joseph chose to wander along byways bright with anemones. Both parents called the child's attention to the beauties of nature, of creation, the handiwork of God. They pointed out how the fig tree bore its fruit in the springtime, how to train the vine that it might produce the finest grapes. They roused his interest in the straying lambs, the circling vultures ready to drop on their prey. They pointed to houses solid because built upon the rock, to fields left barren because of lazy labourers, to the lilies that bloomed only for God's glory, neither sowing nor reaping. They explained why different plants require different kinds of soil and taught him how to recognize the cockle and tares that strangle the wheat. Looking at the sky they showed him how to forecast the weather. It was they from whom he first learned: "When it is evening you say, 'The weather will be fair, for the sky is red.' And in the morning you say, 'It will be stormy today, for the sky is red and lowering'" (Matt 16:2-3). Or again: "When you see a cloud rising in the west, you say at once, 'A shower is coming,' and so it comes to pass. And when you see the south wind blow, you say, 'There will be a scorching heat,' and so it comes to pass" (Luke 12:54-55).

Years later, Jesus used these things to emphasize a point he wished to make. We have a right to wonder what were his thoughts as he listened to Joseph's words, and when we read the parables in the Gospel, we may remember it was from Joseph, in his childhood, he got his experimental knowledge of these things.

23

Joseph taught Jesus

Is not this the carpenter, the son of Mary? (Mark 6:3)

The time has passed when Mary, obliged by her household duties to leave her home for a short time, carried the infant to Joseph for him to care for until her return. And Joseph, as he watched the child playing with the sawdust or the golden curled shavings fallen on the floor, was utterly ravished at the sight.

The time has passed when Jesus went to the Rabbi to school and joined with his small companions in repeating out loud the texts of the Law, pointing with his finger to the words written on the scroll. Nor is it still the time when on returning home in the evening Joseph, taking the child on his knee, in the dim light of the lamp, would have him repeat what he had learned at school and help him prepare the lesson for the next day.

For Jesus has grown up. After having helped his mother for several years in her household duties, he had passed gradually under the tutelage of St Joseph. From then on most of his days were spent in the workshop.

He had begun by watching his father at work. He had been sent to fulfil little commissions. Some easy tasks were confided to him: "Will you please hand me the hammer? Sweep up the sawdust and take it to your mother?" An old etching pictures Joseph late in the evening, planing at his workbench, while the child Jesus stands beside him, holding a lantern so that its rays fall upon the table.

The day finally came when Joseph let him use the tools himself and showed him how best to manipulate them, the large hand covering and carefully guiding the small one.

And under his direction, he who had created the universe as if in play, learned to saw boards, fit parts together, polish wood. And he who would one day say: "Take my yoke upon you ..." (Matt 11:29), would have learned from experience how a yoke is made.

Jesus did nothing without asking Joseph's advice. Never was there in the world an apprentice who listened so carefully, with such docility to his master's teaching.

No one is bound to think that the first objects that came from his hands were perfect. The Creator, on becoming incarnate, first placed himself under the tutelage of a creature. All the same, he was very quick to grasp all the fine points and acquire all the necessary skill. His strong young hands were adept and resourceful in performing a complicated task. He knew just how many blows of the hatchet were needed to shape a yoke, how to square the timber. With ease he wielded the cutter and sledge hammer; skilfully he operated the hempen rope to crank and turn the drill.

Soon, when he asked Joseph, "Father, how should I begin this piece of work?" Joseph would answer, "Do as You think best. I have really nothing more to teach You. You are better than I at the job!"

After that they worked side by side from morning till evening. At dawn they entered the shop. They opened the shutters and sunlight flooded the whole place. Everywhere was the good healthy smell of worked wood. The workbench stood in the centre of the shop. The tools hung from huge hooks on the walls. Sawdust and shavings were swept into a pile in a corner to be taken to Mary in the evening.

They began their preparations by putting on their leather aprons. The heavy cloaks often seen in statues in our churches were cumbersome and were not worn during working hours. They took up their work where the day before they had left off, or began something entirely new.

Joseph's workroom was like any other in that day. Success depended not on electric apparatus but on the strength of a man's arms. A modern carpenter, could he visit the shop at Nazareth, would smile at the primitive setup and the old-fashioned tools.

Their hands were hard and calloused. They sometimes cut themselves on the sharp instruments, and Claudel speaks of "Joseph's fingers often bound with a linen bandage as happens with those who work in wood." And in that case we are sure Mary was the nurse.

They worked ceaselessly to the sound of the monotonous buzzing of saws and the staccato blows of the hammers. The shavings flew and the chips whirled about. With their sleeves they wiped away the beads of sweat gathered on their foreheads.

Together they nailed in place the spokes of a cartwheel. With meticulous care they measured the straight lines of a plank or made a window sash that would exactly fit its frame. Everything was done in the same spirit with which they recited the ritual prayers in the synagogue.

For the most part they worked in silence. Sometimes probably they intoned a psalm, alternately chanting the verses. Could this have been the first recitation of the Divine Office in choir?

Labourers in those days were not limited to eight hours or less of work a day, after which the shop was closed, the doors locked. Claudel again writes somewhere: "Their shop must have been dear to the children of the town as are all carpenter shops." Certainly they played about and were not driven away by him who said: "Let the little ones come to me and forbid them not...."

Passers-by, too, came in gladly. Their tongues were busy telling of the same old grievances, the evils of the times and so on. They brought the two workers up to date on what was going on in the village, the country round about, politics. Jesus and Joseph listened as they went on with their work, losing none of their serenity. Joseph let Jesus do the talking. His words were full of wisdom. They thrilled the visitors, made them think. While showing himself a faithful keeper of the Law, this young apprentice had ideas that often overthrew the narrow preconceived notions to which these people had always clung.

As to the customers, though they had to admit they were satisfied with the work done, they had also –a universal custom in the East–to haggle about the price. The argument was prolonged. They tried to put off paying as long as possible. But Joseph, remembering his responsibility for providing food for his little family, determined to be firm. He demanded what was his due: "What I charge is right and just. We must love justice!"

How little did those men think when they carried away their yokes, their chests, their wheels, that he who had made them had fashioned the dome of heaven.... What would we not give to own some object made by Jesus! It is true, of course, that we have something better: the Wood of the Cross on which on a certain day he stretched himself to perform his greatest work for which all the others had been but a preparation.

Even after sunset Jesus and Joseph worked on– sometimes until very late if some special task needed to be finished. In that case, Mary's figure was silhouetted in the doorway. She began by congratulating them on the beautiful cedar or sycamore furniture they had made. But then she told them their dinner was ready–hot soup steamed on the table. They tried to excuse themselves for not being on time. They had promised to finish this or that for the next day.... They came into the house then, dead tired but happy to be together again. After having used their tools, all day, every day, their hands were stiff and swollen, their backs ached from leaning over the workbench. But now all was well. They were at home with Mary.

There were times when they did not need to go to the workshop. Instead, they went to the forest to cut down some standing timber they had bought. They chose a tree, lopped off the branches, felled the trunk, sawed it into logs. In the Orient, only the most miserably poor do not possess an ass. Joseph must of necessity have owned one in order to carry on his work, and the animal would have helped drag the cut wood back to the shop.

On some days they went to different houses to work. They started out early in the morning to go there where they were expected. Perhaps a floor was to be laid, a heavy chest mended, a frame to be fitted, a door to be hung. They walked in single file, usually in silence, their bag of tools slung over their shoulders, carrying in their hands the package of provisions Mary had prepared for their meal.

It is not unlikely that Joseph was also the owner of a small parcel of land. In an Egyptian document it is mentioned that a certain Pavetis, a carpenter by trade, rented with others a small property where he cultivated what we today would call his allotment. When Jesus later spoke of sowing time and harvest, good earth, stony ground, wheat and cockle, the barren fig tree, prices in the market place, the hen and her chicks, the workers in the vineyard, ploughed furrows, the lilies of the field, he spoke from experience, as one who had known, one who had seen, one who had had a share in cultivating a field or a garden belonging to his family.

It is possible that if no customer needed any carpentry work done, Jesus and Joseph might have gone to the fisheries at what was then called Aricne, a town on the south shore of the Lake of Genesareth not very far from Nazareth, to help pack and nail the great cases and barrels of salted fish.

What seems certain is that far from confining themselves to one trade, they practised several. Father Bernard, the author of *Le Mystere de Jesus,* remarks: "The village or small town artisans remained in close contact with the peasants round about. In general, they were not so taken up with their own trades, nor such specialists in their own jobs as not to be willing to offer a helping hand to the farmers and vine-dressers in times of stress or abundant harvests, in the fields or vineyards or olive orchards."[21]

Jesus could not keep away from men he had come to save, and he gave an example to others by giving himself in their service. He it was who would one day tell the people a parable concerning a good Samaritan. He it was who a few days before his death gave us his last testament: "A new commandment I give you, that you love one another: ... as I have loved you."

---

[21] Vol. 1, p. 227 (Mulhouse: Editions Salvator).

24

Jesus taught Joseph

Jesus advanced in wisdom and age and grace before God and men (Luke 2:52)

The workshop in Nazareth is a prolongation of Bethlehem and a preparation for Calvary. Both teach the same mysterious lesson, or rather the second completes the first. Bethlehem taught the necessity of detachment and renunciation; Nazareth the dignity of labour, its value as a means of sanctification and redemption.

Repeated too often and too carelessly is the declaration that God came into this world, became a manual labourer, in order to choose what was lowest. That statement is inexact and much to be regretted. On the contrary, he came to teach us how great a thing it is to use our arms, our physical powers in the accomplishing of lowly tasks, tasks in his eyes so sacred that he did not consider it beneath his dignity as God to take them upon himself.

By becoming members of the working class, Jesus and Joseph canonized work.

Their workshop on the outside looked like any other of its kind. But the spirit of love which animated the two artisans raised up and sublimated their labour. Each movement of their hands from morning till night became a kind of liturgical service in which they offered and consecrated their whole beings to God the Creator.

Why did Jesus choose for his father a man who worked in wood? Doubtless one reason was because wood, of all created substances, is one of the most widespread and indispensable. It was to be used in our redemption, just as the Church at different times makes use of stone for her altars, water for her sacraments, oil for anointing, wine for the chalice, wheat for the Eucharist.

By means of the wood of the accursed tree in the Garden of Eden we were lost; wood must reappear purified to become the instrument of our salvation. In a wooden manger the Babe of Bethlehem was laid. On Golgotha, a wooden Cross was his resting place. Lying upon it, fastened to it by four great nails, he gave up his life in blood and tears.

In the meantime, during his hidden life at Nazareth, he planed wood, shaping it with love. As his hand felt a wooden beam of oak or cedar or olive to gauge its quality, his gesture became a caress for that creature with whose help he would save the world.

Isaias had prophesied: "A child is born to us, a son is given us; upon his shoulder dominion rests."

That dominion resting on his shoulder was, moment by moment at Nazareth, the beam of wood he carried to his workbench.

Daily, wooden objects he had made left the

shop. His voice one day would ring out: "I am the living bread that has come down from heaven.... He who eats my flesh and drinks my blood has life everlasting...." Wheat and grape will be given supreme honour in his future Church. Ploughshares will cut furrows where the golden grain will grow to be our manna, and the purple grapes ripen to be our drink.

And the two carpenters work serenely in the workshop. They are silent because they have no need of words to speak of the union and harmony between them. They look at each other. Jesus admires this man whom he calls Father; his eyes rest upon him with pleasure; this just man working beside him, with him, his face alight with holiness. Always wise, patient, foreseeing, selfless, devoted; his counsels prevail. His soul is closed to pride; the charity of his heart ceaselessly urges him to do for others. Over and over he says to himself the words of the Spirit on the days of creation: "God saw that all he had made was very good" (Gen 1:31). And Jesus saw that Joseph was God's masterpiece. He thanked his heavenly Father for the moral and religious grandeur hidden in this just man, whose docile soul, responsive to grace, fitted him perfectly for his mission.

In the workshop, Jesus was the apprentice and Joseph the master. Yet often the master looked to the apprentice to learn from him. As he saw him bending over the workbench, he remembered the words of the angel of the Annunciation to Mary: "He shall be great, and shall be called the Son of the Most High; and the Lord God will give him the throne of David his father, and he shall be king over the house of Jacob forever; and of his kingdom there shall be no end" (Luke 1:32-33). And he is a bit disconcerted to see this "Son of the Most High" a poor carpenter, earning his living in the village. Without knowing exactly what his mission among men was to be, Joseph guessed that what he was now doing was somehow related to his later work and to the name he himself at God's command had given him: "Jesus, Saviour".

The prophets' themes had been the same–among them especially Isaias and Zacharias (Is 42:2-4; Zach 9:9). In announcing the Messiah they had spoken of the gentleness, the humility, the meekness of this Chosen One of Yahweh who would not cry out, who would not raise his voice in the streets, who would not break the bruised reed nor quench the smoking flax.

Joseph did not speak to Jesus of his astonishment at his not making himself known to the world at once. Time was passing and nothing connected with salvation seemed to be happening. He knew that whatever was, was wise and just. Once again he surrendered himself to the will of God.

Mary lived longer with Jesus than did Joseph who, as we shall see, probably died before the beginning of the Public Life. But in the meantime, Joseph was the more favoured. From morning till evening he lived with him in closest intimacy. He worked with him. They took their meals together, slept in the same room, prayed together.

Like the tree planted near the running brook of which the Psalmist sings, whose leaves stayed green and whose fruits never failed, Joseph lived always at the source of all grace, all life. His faith grew stronger and stronger, his love deeper and deeper. The Gospels opened out before his eyes in a manner familiar, continual, concrete.

Even before Jesus' birth his love for him had become fruitful, watered by his anguished tears. It had increased with every care he bestowed upon him, with every fear suffered for him, with every privation undergone for him, with the protection with which he surrounded him during the years of exile. Now, when Jesus was no longer a child and had no need of that kind of devotedness, and had become the close companion of his daily life, he tried only to make his own will absolutely one with his.

Joseph fed his own spiritual life on what he saw, on what he heard. Nothing was allowed to escape him. He kept the memory of all things as precious treasures in his heart and mind. He lived only for Jesus. He had no desires apart from Jesus.

He was there, near him; that was enough. In him the programme given to the Philippians by St Paul was realized: *Mihi vivere Christus est*–My life is summed up in the one word–Christ.

And in the measure in which Christ revealed himself to Joseph, his obedience to God became more perfect. Like Jesus himself, his food and drink was the Father's will.

25

The "trinity" at Nazareth

And these three are one (1 John 5:7)

Far from being renowned in any way, Nazareth was a poor, straggling little hamlet, very old certainly, but without a history. So true was this that its insignificance was made a mockery of in the well-known proverb: "Can any good come out of Nazareth?"

The village was perched on a rounded hillside. Its houses were surrounded by barley and wheat fields, gardens and vineyards. Withdrawn from the much frequented roads, travellers ignored or scorned it.

The most plausible derivation of its name is En-Nazira, meaning the guardian; but a tradition coming down from St Jerome says the name signified "City of Flowers". It is true that its springtime beauty made it look like a vast bouquet of many-coloured flowers.

Its steep roads were no more than narrow twisting passages. Many of its houses at that time, like some even today, were dug out of the hillside. It was in such a house, exactly like that of their neighbours, the Holy Family lived. The roofed-over front was supported by masonry, but the greater part was carved out of the limestone rock. There were no more than two or three rooms. The largest was that near the should be last, and the last should take the first place. God thereby teaches the lesson that power is less a privilege than a means of service.

Joseph was the representative of divine authority. He knew himself to be far removed from his wife and son in dignity, and at the thought of the distance that separated him from God and from the most elevated of his creatures, his soul trembled. However when time and circumstance demanded the exercise of his authority, he neither hesitated nor wavered.

And it was with absolute spontaneity that Mary and Jesus turned to him as the one appointed by God to be their head. Through him God spoke to them. They well knew that through his means they could know and fulfil the Father's will.

However, in giving orders to Jesus, Mary and Joseph looked upon him as their master and model. Such holiness they felt in him that they were powerfully and instinctively carried forward to imitate him. He was the mirror of their ideal. They sought to stamp themselves with the seal of his perfection, as later on he said he was himself marked with his Father's seal. "He who sees me, sees also the Father."

All three led a hidden life. In the eyes of their fellows they were looked upon merely as pious, fervent Israelites, faithful keepers of the Law. Their conduct was edifying, but all the same their religious practices were never singular nor exaggerated. Nothing on the outside would have led anyone to guess the overflowing richness of their souls. So perfectly did they keep God's secret that those nearest to them, their own relatives, never discerned in Jesus the Word Incarnate.

Living in obscurity, they did not dream of seeking any special privileges or marks of esteem. Their life indeed seemed so ordinary, so uneventful that neither history nor the Evangelists can tell us anything about it. It looks in fact as if in their Gospels these writers had determined to pass over in silence anything they had learned of the life of the Holy Family in Nazareth.

We are tempted to complain a bit about this: "Lord, did You not tell us it is not right to put one's light under a bushel? Why did You wait so long to show Yourself? And if You wanted to keep hidden, why did You not let the world know something of those whom You called father and mother?"

Someday the appointed time for the revelation would come. Meanwhile, before preaching, it is good to give an example. Before teaching–silence, self-effacement, abnegation, humility–Jesus, and others who plough the first furrows, must show those near them what is meant by these virtues. The world must learn that what is most profitable, most valuable, most impregnated with the Gospel is without glamour, but consists in the accomplishment of daily, hidden work.

The rhythm of life of the Holy Family was no different, then, from that of their neighbours in Nazareth.

In the Book of Proverbs it is written concerning the valiant woman: "She rises while it is still night, and distributes food to her household." And so it was with Mary. She prepares places for Jesus and Joseph at table; she serves them; she even worries a little about the amount of work they have to do. It is Joseph, according to custom, who blesses the food, breaks the bread and drinks first from the cup.

Then after the two carpenters have left for their workshop, Mary puts the house in order, sweeps the rooms, grinds the wheat, goes to the well for water, to the market for food. When she returns from the village, she kneads the dough, lights the fire and bakes the loaves. When her husband and son come home at noon, their meal is ready for them.

At sundown, Mary stands at the door or goes a little way along the road to meet them. She tells them how glad she is to have them back. She looks lovingly at their toughened, calloused hands grown strong and hard in labouring for her.

As for them. They give her the money they have earned during the day. Not very much probably, because sympathetic as they are, conscientious about their work, people abuse their kindness and honesty. But Mary smiles. She tells them it is quite enough for their simple needs; she can even relieve the distress of certain people she knows, who are sick or very old or in want.

And then in the evening hours spent together in intimate and sweet companionship, in which each one feels joyful at being with those he loves, they raise their hearts to God, uniting in a prayer of thanksgiving and praise.

This is the hour of religious discussion when Mary and Joseph listen avidly to Jesus. These two he loves are the first to hear the substance of the good news the Evangelists will make known by their writing to the whole world.

And when the hour grows late and they prepare to go to rest, using almost the same words as the disciples of Emmaus, Mary and Joseph say to each other: "Were not our hearts burning within us when he opened to us the Scriptures?"

26

Joseph's last years

*Joseph is a growing son, a growing son
and comely to behold* (Gen 49:22)

The Patriarch Jacob, feeling his death approaching, called his sons to his bedside. Before blessing them he uttered a prophecy concerning them and told each one what he foresaw would be his special destiny. When the turn came of Joseph, his favourite, with burning ardour he reminded him of the prodigies he had accomplished in Egypt, the height to which he had risen under Pharaoh, and he cried out that Joseph whom he had seen grow so great, would go greater still, would never cease to grow.

These words of the dying Jacob are applied by the Church to the son of another Jacob, the humble carpenter of Nazareth. The growth spoken of concerns the progress of the honour and reverence paid him, the special mission with which the Church entrusts him, and the growing understanding of his spiritual life which she unrolls before our eyes.

Before being raised to the dignity of the husband of Mary, he had already been given the title of "just". Now where did this "justice" daily increase if not in the atmosphere of the home at Nazareth?

The nearer anyone is physically and morally to the source of holiness, the more grace he receives. Now Joseph had constantly before his eyes the spotless perfection of Mary and the increased holiness of the Man-God. The contact with their super-eminent virtues meant of necessity a constant growth in holiness in him.

The Gospel tells us that at the mere approach of Mary, John the Baptist was sanctified while still in his mother's womb. Equally flooded with grace must Joseph have been, Joseph who lived always under the rays of the "Sun of Justice" and of her who, having borne him, had been at the same instant commissioned to carry on that same beneficent work of sanctification in the world.

When the Child Jesus put his arms around Joseph's neck in a loving embrace, must not that manifestation of affection have been accompanied by a closer participation in Divine Life? Then as Jesus was growing up and Joseph was more and more in close contact with him, the outpouring of love and light must have abundantly increased.

Though externally Joseph's life was passed in silence and self-effacement, those very qualities made him astonishingly expendable. As a result of having submitted perfectly to the exigencies of the Divine will, of having corresponded generously and unreservedly to the inspirations of grace, he belonged, more than others, to that family of souls of good will called blessed by the angels in Bethlehem.

While the only ideal, the absorbing preoccupation of many men is to seek to appear, to shine, to make their mark in the world, Joseph had but one ambition: to fulfil his mission, to carry out his appointed task in perfect dependence on the Father in heaven.

He set himself to throw light on the present by means of the past. He liked to remind himself of all the gifts he had received, of all he had heard and seen, of the ways by which God had led him through sorrow and joy to perfect peace.

Those Christians who want to penetrate into the mystery which is Joseph will find in his life, as in that of Mary, a series of seven joys and seven sorrows. As this book nears its end, it is well to slip through our fingers the rosary of those mysteries etched by God on his soul.

The first was his indescribable anguish when he saw in his betrothed the signs of approaching motherhood. His heart was torn at the thought of losing her, but when the angel had assured him that her fruitfulness was of the Holy Spirit, the frightful nightmare was changed into a song of praise to God, a redoubled respect and tenderness for her.

A second time his heart was pierced as by a sword when at the birth of Jesus all the doors in Bethlehem were closed against him and he had to shelter Mary in a stable. But how joyful was the compensation when Mary had put the new-born infant into his arms and he had pressed him against his heart, knelt in adoration before his crib and seen those sent by God, the shepherds and the Magi, do as he.

The third sword thrust came when as father of the child he had been obliged to circumcise the infant and cause the tears of pain and the blood of the wound to flow. But then, at the same moment it was he, Joseph, who was the first to pronounce the name of Jesus he imposed on the child—that name which through all ages men would lovingly repeat over and over again. Enlightened on the meaning of that name, he foresaw the work of salvation to be wrought through the blood of this Little One.

The old man Simeon was the cause of the fourth sorrow when, drawing back the veil of the future, he announced that Jesus would be a sign of contradiction to men, and that Mary's own heart would one day be transfixed. But a joy, too, followed and consoled Joseph: Jesus would be the light of all nations and the glory of Israel.

The fulfilment of Simeon's prophecy was not long in coming, for Joseph's fifth sorrow was the flight into Egypt. Like hunted beast, to save Jesus from Herod's fury, the Holy Family fled through the desert into exile. But the desert itself flowered for Joseph, since he could pour himself out in service for the two he loved.

Hardly had they returned to Palestine when he learned that Archelaus, as cruel and bloodthirsty as his father, ruled in Judea. He dared not return to Bethlehem. A sixth sorrow. But his anxiety was turned to joy when the angel of the Annunciation came again as ambassador from heaven to tell him to take Jesus and Mary to Nazareth and settle there once more in their happy home.

The seventh sword pierced Joseph's heart when he thought he had lost Jesus in Jerusalem and when for three days he sought him with indescribable anguish, conjuring up with what perils he might be threatened. But what joy on finding him! his love then was enriched as a result of his suffering during the days in which they had been separated.

Such were Joseph's memories. Trials indeed had not been wanting, but God had blessed him with overwhelming joys.

He rehearsed in his heart the words Tobias had heard: "Because you were acceptable to God, it was necessary for temptation to prove you" (Tob 12:13). Far from fretting, he had made use of his crucifying sufferings to grow in virtue and strengthen his loving fidelity.

As for his joys he told his God that they were far beyond his merits; that he had been treated with divine munificence; that his life could not be long enough to render proper thanks. He was God's servant, well content to carry out his designs; well content to leave this earth when such should be his good pleasure.

27

The death of the good servant

"Lord, now you are dismissing your servant in peace, according to your word; for my eyes have seen your salvation which you have prepared in the presence of all peoples" (Luke 2:29-31).

As so little space is devoted to St Joseph in the Gospels, and as no information is given about his birth, so is there none about his death. He is never mentioned except when his life casts some light on the life of Jesus. Only from the time of his betrothal to Mary until his adopted son has become an adult is there need to speak of him.

If, consequently, we are to speak of Joseph's death, we must add to the Evangelists' accounts in order to find beyond their silence those probabilities on which light is cast by centuries of Christian meditation.

We know nothing of his death, neither the time nor the circumstances, but all writers agree that Joseph died before Jesus began his public ministry. This fact is implied in the Gospel. When the aged Simeon revealed the future at the Presentation in the Temple, it was to Mary alone he spoke of the sword that would pierce her heart. Had Simeon foreseen that

Joseph, Mary's spouse, would also be present at that supreme trial would he not have associated him with her in his prophetic words?

No. Joseph was not present at the time or place of Christ's Passion. Had he, her faithful support for years, been there, then Jesus would surely not have confided his mother to St John.

Moreover, Joseph never appears nor is mention made of him during the Public Life of the Messiah. The Galileans, nevertheless, spoke of Jesus as the carpenter's son, implying that not sufficient time had elapsed since Joseph's death to allow one who had been considered as his father to have been forgotten.

Joseph's presence at the time when Jesus was preaching might indeed have caused misunderstanding among Christ's hearers. His constant use of the words "my Father" would almost certainly have led to some confusion of thought.

So far as we know, it was not of old age that Joseph died. Since he may be considered to have been but a little older than Mary at the time of their marriage, he could not have been over sixty at the time of his death.

But he was worn out from his ceaseless labours. Little by little Jesus had taken over the hardest work in the workshop, leaving to Joseph the lighter tasks. Anxious care and Mary's devoted attention put off for only a time his departure from this earth.

One evening on returning home Joseph, who never complained, had to admit that he was very tired. His head ached, his limbs were stiff, his body cold,

his heartbeat weak. Jesus and Mary helped him to lie
down on his straw mat and stayed at his side doing
what they could to lighten his sufferings.

Joseph realized that the time had come for him
to go. As always, he who had never had a wish but to
do the will of his Lord whose servant he was, abandoned himself completely to Divine Wisdom.

He welcomed his illness as he had welcomed all
the manifestations of God's will. He saw it as a messenger sent from God, his Lord and Master, who had
appointed the hour for his departure. To die was a
supreme means of rendering service and worship to
that Lord.

He saw that his work was finished. He knew he
had tried as best he could to do it well. The Eternal
Father had confided to him the Word Incarnate and
his mother as their protector and father. He had pro-
vided them not with luxury or riches, but by God's
help with what was necessary. For a long time now
the apprentice had needed no help from him. His son
was the master carpenter.

Because he was Joseph he realized too that his
presence might become an obstacle rather than a help
to Jesus. The world must not believe any longer that
he was Jesus' true father.

He had never asked his adopted son any questions about the time and manner of his manifestation.
Perhaps he had been surprised that Jesus' life had
been so ordinary–that of an unknown workman. But
he knew too that this could not go on. The time must
soon come when Jesus would reveal himself to the

world as the one sent by God, the Messiah.

"Yes," he said, "it is good, it is right that I should go."

Then, recalling Simeon's farewell canticle, he repeated the verses so fitting at this moment:

"Now, O Lord, I your servant may depart in peace. I have guarded the ineffable secret. For myself I have kept nothing. I have turned nothing to my own profit. I have never opposed your designs. My eyes have not seen the full manifestation of salvation promised the world. In the Messiah I have seen only humility and hiddenness. Until now his life like mine has been passed in a carpenter's workshop. As yet he has not begun his mission, he who is the Saviour of the world and the Light of all nations. Those revelations are not for me, but I have seen enough to sing the *Magnificat* my wife has taught me. I have taken part in the sowing. It is enough for me to know that the harvest is near. It is best that for the reaping I shall not be there, for men will then more easily believe that Jesus has no father according to the flesh."

All these thoughts must have come to his mind even though he did not put them into words. He was so accustomed to be silent so that God might speak, that he felt his silence before death should not be broken. St Francis de Sales places the following words on his lips: "O my child, my Jesus, as your heavenly Father gave your body into my hands the day you came into the world, so on the day I leave the world I give my soul into your hands."

Quietly, silently, leaving no last word, no will,

no testament, he prepared for death. The sacrament for the dying had not yet been instituted. For him there was neither Viaticum nor the Anointing of the Sick, but he had near him the Source of grace and the Mediatrix of grace, both pouring out upon him their immense love and tender gratitude.

In his celebrated work on St Joseph, Father Patrignani, contemplating this deathbed, uses these words: "You had ever beside your couch Jesus and Mary, each vying with the other to render you the services you had rendered them during your life. In their turn they gave you to drink; they proffered every help their poverty permitted. Jesus strengthened you with words of eternal life; Mary consoled you by all the tender care her great love could suggest. How often did Jesus' cool hand rest upon your head. How often did Mary moisten your dry lips. Ah! most surely, great Saint, you died of love upheld to the end by the Son of God, consoled by the Mother of God."

Jesus' arms were about him in those last moments. He told him the separation would not be for long. Soon they would see each other again. Joseph hung on his words as he told him of the eternal banquet to which the Father was calling him: "Good and faithful servant, the time of service is over and gone. You are entering the house of God to receive your reward. For I was hungry and you gave me to eat. I was thirsty and you gave me to drink. I was homeless and you took me in; naked and you clothed me."

And he, who during all his life had run counter to Lucifer, who had had one only thought and desire–

to serve his Lord–slept like a child in the kiss of God.

Because such a death is perfect, peaceful, happy, because he died in the arms of Jesus and Mary, the Sovereign Pontiffs, especially Pius IX, Leo XIII and Benedict XV, confirmed what Christian piety had so long held, and presented St Joseph to faithful Christians as the patron of the dying. They urged all to call upon him to deliver them from the danger of everlasting death and to obtain for them that their return to the Lord of life might be peaceful and joyful as was his own.

Jesus and Mary closed his eyes, anointed and wrapped his body in linen cloths sprinkled with myrrh. A little later, their heads covered by their cloaks, they followed the bier borne on the shoulders of young men to the place of burial.

During the public life, Jesus wept for the dead Lazarus. How many tears must he not have shed for his foster father Joseph; and those who now saw him weep spoke the words of those others at Bethany: "See how he loved him!"

The people of Nazareth followed in the funeral procession. His relatives, his neighbours, his customers were there. What praise they had for this just man, whose only ambition was to honour God and show respect for his neighbours. They spoke of his life, which in itself had been a condemnation of pride and selfishness; of this silent man, who had never said an unkind word to or about anyone; of this meek and gentle man who had never borne a grudge, never taken part in political quarrels; of this descendant of

entrance which served as the common room where
the meals were taken. Behind this, a passage or cur-
tained opening led into what was probably Mary's
room. Over the opening of the cave proper, a kind of
terrace surrounded by a low wall was reached by an
outside stairway.

There was no luxury and very little comfort to be
found in such dwellings. Straw mats were scattered on
the hard earthen floor. The wooden furniture was
simple, like that of the people round about: bedrolls,
clothes chests, household utensils, pitchers, a hand
mill for grinding wheat, a rug or two, and cushions
for visitors.

In this poor little home there were only, says
Paul Claudel, "Three people who loved one another,
and it was they who were to change the face of the
earth." They were three, but the love which filled
them, which never lessened but became each day
more intense, more strong, more tender, united them
in a oneness which was, in a way, like the Blessed
Trinity—of which St John wrote: "And these three are
one: and the three form but one." Their love made of
their souls, one soul; of their hearts, one heart. They
were in communion one with another at every instant.

In dignity they were not equal, but the hierarchical order chosen by God was faithfully kept. Joseph
was totally submitted to the Divine Will; Mary to
Joseph, and Jesus to both Mary and Joseph. Pre-
eminence was in inverse order to excellence of value.
The least in greatness was first in authority. The
Evangelical law laid down that he who would be first

David, who reduced to poverty had accepted his lowly condition without complaint.

Jesus and Mary then returned to their home; without Joseph how very empty it seemed to them. As custom required, they left the door open for eight days in order to welcome their friends and relations who came to sympathize with them and offer condolences.

Joseph's soul entered Limbo to proclaim to the Just, who had been waiting since the beginning of the world, their approaching entrance into the Paradise of God. With full knowledge he could say to them: "Your deliverance is at hand. The Redeemer is on earth. Soon the doors of heaven will be opened to you!"

And the Just exulted with joy and gratitude. They surrounded Joseph and intoned that paean of praise which for all the centuries to come would never cease:

Blessed be you who have announced to us the coming of the Saviour!

Blessed be Emmanuel whom you have carried in your arms!

Blessed be Mary ever Virgin your beloved spouse!

28

Glorious St Joseph

Since God has made all this known to you, ... you shall be in charge of my palace (Gen. 41:39, 40)

There is not even a tradition concerning Joseph's burial place, nor is there any spot where his relics are venerated. Silent in life, silent in death, he was stripped of all things not essential to true glory.

He, above all, was that saint who understood, as Bossuet says, "That to be hidden in Christ Jesus is of all glories the greatest." He had sought not what the world admires, but what was pleasing to his Lord. If in effacing himself before the Divine will he had already procured for himself the greatest of joys, these were only a prelude to the marvellous rewards with which God would crown him. According to his self-abasement, so would his exaltation be. Because he did not try to appear before men, he would be glorified in their sight. Because he loved to be hidden and unknown, God would make his light shine for all the world to see. But God wished to leave to men to discover his greatness, to become ever more aware of his radiance as if to prove in his case the truth of Jacob's prophecy concerning that other Joseph of the Old Testament: *Joseph accrescens*– Joseph destined to be raised on high.

After his death Mary surely spoke to St John and the other Apostles of him who had surrounded her with such devoted care, whom she had loved with such virginal tenderness. It might be said that the first panegyrics on St Joseph were preached by Mary.

Yet devotion to him in the early Christian Church was non-existent, or at least no trace of it can be found. His name and memory were wrapped in obscurity. That silence so complete in his earthly life seemed to be continued in his heavenly life as if nothing concerning him was ever to be known.

This apparent censure is easily explained. As the Church was then still in a state of struggle and formation, it was essential that before devotion to the spouse of Mary could be promulgated it was necessary that her virginity be recognized and revered, and at the same time the divinity of her Son be well established. In favouring devotion to St Joseph, the Church feared there might arise misunderstandings; that honour paid to him might be taken as honour paid to the father of Jesus according to the flesh.

It would seem, too, that while early Christianity was paying homage to certain other saints, especially to the Precursor John, to the Apostles, and to the first martyrs, St Joseph appeared to have been forgotten. All the same, in the homilies of the great Doctors his name and his office as foster father of Jesus are often mentioned. Especially in the works of Origen, of St Gregory of Nazianzen, of St John Chrysostom and, above all, of St Augustine, is to be found the seed of the mystical theology concerning him which was to flourish later on. The darkness was not total, although the praise accorded him did not include prayers for his intercession.

The long delay served but to enhance with greater splendour the field of glory on which one day he was to be crowned. The time came when God could no longer allow one to whom he had shown such deference while on earth to remain longer in obscurity.

In the 12th century, St Bernard directed minds and hearts toward the holy patriarch by emphasizing his matchless holiness. He did not as yet urge the faithful to invoke Joseph's assistance, but by highlighting his virtues, Bernard laid down the foundation of the future devotion Christians were to have for him.

Then came the great heralds of this devotion. In the 14th century, Cardinal Pierre D'Ailly composed the first theological treatise on St Joseph. His disciple, Gerson, chancellor of the University of Paris, in a rigorous doctrinal thesis, enumerated the reasons men had for honouring the saint. Later, the Franciscan, Bernardine of Siena, the great preacher of the 15th century, Isidore of Isolanis of the 16th century, and still more the reformer of Carmel, St Teresa of Avila, in the same century, all contributed by their great influence, their teachings, their writings and their example to make the devotion popular.

From that time on, the honour paid by Christians to St Joseph has never ceased to grow and be enriched. It looks as if the Church wished to repay with interest the tribute of honour she was so long in according him.

The Apostolic Letter *Inclytum Patriarchum* of July 7, 1871, contains this declaration of Pius IX: "The Roman Pontiffs, our predecessors, in order to increase and rouse in the hearts of the faithful greater devotion and reverence for the holy Patriarch, and to urge them to have recourse with greater confidence to his powerful intercession with God, must make use of ,whenever possible, and under new forms, all approved signs of public veneration.

Among the Pontiffs it is enough to mention Sixtus IV who inserted the feast of Saint Joseph in the Roman breviary and missal; Gregory XV who, on May 8, 1621, decreed that the feast should be celebrated in the whole world as a double; Clement X, who on December 6, 1670, raised the feast to a double of second class; Clement XI who by the decree of February 4, 1714, enriched the feast with a Mass and Office proper to it; and lastly, Benedict XIII who on December 19, 1726, ordered that the name of Saint Joseph should be inserted in the litanies of the saints."

It was again Pius IX who in the second year of his pontificate extended to the Universal Church by special indult of the Holy See the feast of the Patronage of St Joseph, already celebrated in certain places. Then, in answer to innumerable petitions which came to him from all over the world, on December 8, 1870, he solemnly declared St Joseph to be the Patron of the Universal Church. The decree reads: "As God established the Patriarch Joseph, son of Jacob, as governor over all Egypt to guarantee wheat to preserve the lives of the people, so at the time appointed for the redemption of the world, he chose another Joseph of whom the former was a figure. He named him prince and lord over his house and his possessions and to him entrusted his most precious treasures."

Leo XIII, on his side, in the encyclical dated August 15, 1889, *Quanquam Pluries*, pointed out the special reasons why Joseph was designated to protect the Church.

The patronage confided to Joseph came to him by right because of the functions he had once exercised toward Jesus and Mary in the household of Nazareth. As he was appointed by God to be the provider and defender of the Holy Family and guardian of the Son of God and of his mother, so the Church found there, the root, the foundation for her statement. In heaven most certainly he would carry on in his perfected mission that which he had begun on earth.

Over the Body of Christ which is the Church, as once over the body of the Infant Christ, he would keep watch; he would see to its growth and protect it from its enemies.

Today, as a matter of fact, the devotion to St Joseph is flourishing. There are only few chapels or churches in which there is not an altar dedicated to him, or at least a statue of him. It is impossible to number the religious houses, hospitals, institutions, colleges placed under his protection. A day of the week is consecrated to him, Wednesday; a month, March. More and more Christians have such devotion toward him that they make generous sacrifices in order that still greater glory may accrue to him in the bosom of the Church. Requests pour into Rome, begging that his name be mentioned in the Confiteor after Mary's, and also that mention be made of him in the Canon of the Mass.[22]

The triumphal progress of the humble Joseph is built on the prophetic words once uttered, in Egypt, by Pharaoh addressing his prime minister: "Since God has made all this known to you, there is no one as intelligent and prudent as you; you shall be in charge of my palace and all my people shall obey your commands....

Taking the signet ring from his own hand, he put it on Joseph's. He dressed him in linen robes, and put a chain of gold around his neck. He had him ride in his second chariot. And they all cried out before him 'Bow down' " (Gen 41:39, 43).

---

[22] At the closing of the first session of the Second Vatican Council, Pope John XXIII announced that the name of St Joseph would be included in the Canon (Publisher's note).

29

After Mary, the greatest saint

Pharaoh ... Had him ride in his second chariot.
And they all cried out before him, "Bow down"
(Gen 41:43)

Common ground was made among the theologians after the 16th century in order to compare the grandeur of St Joseph with that of the other saints so that they might be able to define with precision what place he held in the assembly of those crowned by God in heaven.

Often in their discussions they came back on the text of St Gregory Nazianzen who centuries earlier had written: "The Lord united in Joseph as in a sun whatever light and splendour the others possessed."

No one doubts that when God appoints any soul to carry out a certain mission, he endows that soul with all the gifts necessary to accomplish that mission. There has never been any higher calling–after that of Mary, Mother of the Word–any calling equal to that of Joseph, adopted father of Christ and husband of his mother. It must be said, frankly, that next to Mary no creature came nearer to the Man-God and consequently possessed sanctifying grace to the same degree.

Leo XIII in his Encyclical *Quanquam Pluries* echoed this opinion: "Certain it is that the dignity of Mother of God is so exalted that it cannot be surpassed. Nevertheless, since she and Joseph were united in the bond of marriage, there can be no question but that he came nearer than any one else to that super-eminent dignity which places Mary far above all human creatures."

Since he carried in his arms the One who is the heart and soul of the Church, he may be said to be above Peter on whom Christ declared he would build his Church.

For having lived about thirty years in intimate union with Christ, in constant meditation on his life, his eminence surpasses that of St Paul to whom such sublime mysteries were revealed. Greater, too, than John the Evangelist whose privilege it was to lean once on the breast of Jesus, while Joseph time and time again had listened to the beatings of that infant heart; and than also the Apostles, who only spread abroad that name which Joseph had imposed on Jesus.

It might appear more difficult to place him above John the Baptist because of Christ's words: "Amen I say to you, among those born of women there has not risen a greater than John the Baptist." The difficulty is easily met. When speaking thus, Jesus was comparing John to the prophets of the Old Testament, who announced his future coming, while the Baptist's announcement declared him already come and pointed him out to the people. We might say, too, that those words of Jesus were intended to compare John, the greatest prophet of the Old Testament, with that new grandeur which confers on the elect the call to the Kingdom of heaven, that kingdom of which the Church on earth is the foundation, and for that reason he adds: "*Qui minor est in regno coelorum major est illo.*" This may be translated: "Howsoever great the grandeur of John the Baptist who closes the Old Testament, it sinks into insignificance before that of the lowliest Christian."

The doctrine of St Joseph's pre-eminence among the saints is today guaranteed by the most weighty probabilities. It tends to become the common teaching of the Church.[23] On this point the declaration of Leo XIII already cited is especially revealing.

Other problems concerning the outstanding privileges of St Joseph in his connection with our Lady are at present being discussed by eminent theologians. But the affirmative conclusions arrived at will be, in any case, based on irrefutable arguments.

There is no question, of course, of thinking that Joseph from his conception was free from original sin. There are those, however, who think he was sanctified from his birth. If some saints, they say, have had that privilege–Jeremias, John the Baptist, for example– could it have been withheld from the spouse of Mary, predestined as he was to surpass all those others? That is the opinion held by Gerson, St Alphonsus Liguori and many other theologians. They

---

[23] See *Dictionnaire de théologie*, t. 8, col 1516

hold that the mission of the adopted father of Jesus, which placed him so near the Redeemer, made it necessary that he be sanctified before his birth.

Those theologians who hold a different opinion offer the objection that as holiness from birth was an exceptional grace given only for the common good, such holiness was not necessary for St Joseph before his birth, because his appointed office began actually only when he became affianced to Mary. Suarez's quite reasonable conclusion is that the theory of the pre-sanctification of the spouse of Mary, since it is not derived from any scriptural text, must depend on reasons whose value springs from the authority of the majority of the Fathers of the Church, which is here not the case.

Opinions are also divided on the question as to whether concupiscence of the flesh in Joseph was non-existent or was held in check or deadened by a special grace in so far as not to allow for the commission of any sin, even venial. There again, in our opinion, this was not the case. It is a theory not supported by reason and one that cannot be proved. To concede that such a special, absolute, complete privilege might be given is not impossible even where the stain of original sin existed, but it cannot be theologically demonstrated.

All that can be absolutely affirmed is that Joseph, confirmed in grace after his marriage to Mary, profiting from the constant companionship of her who was conceived immaculate, having never resisted the call of grace, saw that supernatural treasure ever growing in his soul. He had been able, in so far as man is capable thereof, of raising himself to so high a degree of perfection that sin had no part in him.

Certain authors, among them Suarez, St Bernardine of Siena, St Francis de Sales, and Bossuet, and even certain Fathers of the Church, are convinced that Joseph ranks among those saints of whom the Evangelist speaks (Matt. 27:52-53), who, rising from their graves after the death of Jesus, revealed themselves to many in Jerusalem.

St Thomas says that their resurrection was definitive and absolute. St Francis de Sales goes so far as to write: "If it is true, as we must believe, that in virtue of our reception of the Blessed Sacrament, our bodies will rise on the day of judgement, how could we possibly doubt that our Saviour took with him to heaven, in body and soul, the glorious Saint Joseph whose honour and grace it had been to carry him so often in his arms, and in whom he was so well pleased? Saint Joseph, then, soul and body is in heaven. About this there can be no cavil or doubt."

Those who hold this opinion adduce the argument that Jesus, choosing an escort of risen souls to emphasize his Resurrection and add to his glorious triumph, could not but number among them and place in the first rank his own adopted father. Besides, were Joseph not body and soul in heaven, the glorious Holy Family would be wanting in its exalted membership.

These are doubtless quite reasonable speculations, but they are impossible to verify. We may or may not choose to affirm or deny them. The contrary opinion is held by some who are convinced that the only glorified bodies in heaven are those of our Lord and his Blessed Mother.

As for the title of "Co-Redemptor" which certain men wish to attribute to St Joseph, their efforts on this score are injudicious. "Co-Redemptor" as applied to St Joseph is to be taken only in the way it is applicable to all those who chose to unite their merits and sufferings to those of Jesus Christ, in order, as St Paul says, "to fill up those things that are wanting to the Passion of Christ." For Joseph, of course, the title used in this sense would have a more exact meaning since he had guarded, nourished and cherished the Divine Victim with the Cross in view. He had by anticipation offered him in the Temple as his own gift, and for Jesus' sake he had endured sufferings whose propitiatory merits have profited all humanity redeemed by the blood of Christ.

Finally, it is not necessary in order to extol St Joseph's greatness to pile up titles of an exceptional order. It is enough, remembering the self-effacement in which he took pleasure, to recall the words of Jesus himself. "Whoever, therefore, humbles himself as this little child, he is the greatest in the kingdom of heaven."

30

The model for Christians

*"We come to you in our afflictions,
O blessed Joseph ... in order that helped by your
example and intercession, we may live in a holy
way"* (Prayer of Leo XIII to St Joseph)

Our ancestors, perhaps realizing better than us
God's interest in every least detail concerning us and
our destiny, set themselves to study the name of
Joseph.[24] They noticed that all the letters in his name
pointed to the saint's outstanding virtues: J for Justice,
O for Obedience, S for Silence, E for Experience, P
for Prudence, H for Humility. We might be tempted to
smile at such childlike simplicity except for the fact
that actually the virtues enumerated do give the
characteristics of soul that Christian tradition has
attributed to him.

All the evangelical perfections, admirably bal-
anced, are to be found in St Joseph, revealed by a
serenity that seems in itself an outpouring of Divine
Wisdom.

The place of honour is held by obedience. Each

---

[24] See especially Isidore of Isolano, *The Sum of Saint Joseph's Gifts,* Vol. 1, p.
60, 2nd ed

time the Evangelist mentions the saint it is to show him practising that virtue. "Rising up, he did as he was commanded." "He rose up", an expression that in Biblical language expresses the promptitude, the energy with which one gives himself to the task he is about to perform.

Joseph appears before us as that servant of whom God can ask anything, like the centurion in the Gospel who said of his servant, "'Go,' and he goes; ... 'Come,' and he comes; ... 'Do this,' and he does it."

As yet the *Our Father* had not been taught to men; yet during his whole life Joseph was endlessly repeating the central phrase, "Father, may your will be done." He had perfectly understood that the greatest wisdom a creature can possess is to live in dependence on his Creator, like the Son who on entering the world offered himself as a complete oblation, "Behold, I come, O Father, to do thy will!"

At every manifestation of a desire from heaven, Joseph surrendered himself like a docile child, ready to answer to every call, every undertaking, every sacrifice. The whole ordering of his life he had placed in the hands of God. He listened always, always he obeyed. He did not know where God would lead him; it was enough that God knew. Never once was he wanting in submission. He did not argue; he did not look back; he did not object; he did not ask for explanations. To be treated with no consideration, to be given no hint beforehand did not cause him to acquiesce less promptly. Nothing, nothing until the very end, held him back.

Obedience is the achievement of the strong and humble. Only God could plumb the depths of Joseph's humility. Because of his mission he knew himself to be favoured by God as none before or after him, but he was neither cast down nor elated by his vocation. He never dreamed of carving out a niche for himself in the great mystery of the Incarnation which dominates the history of all ages. He did not make use of his title of adopted father of the Son of God to set himself apart or on a pedestal. Where others might have sunned themselves in the pleasant glow of pride, he, in the spirit of the *Magnificat* he knew so well, chose but to bury himself more deeply in the shadows.

If he found any good in himself, he recognized it as a free gift from God. Only by his modesty and self-effacement was he distinguished from others. Even with more truth than Elizabeth was he able to say, "From where does this happiness come to me that my God and the Mother of my God have deigned to live in my house?" And with more reason than John the Baptist: "Jesus must increase, I must decrease."

His only pride then lay in fulfilling God's designs, quietly, peacefully, so silently that the Evangelist can give us no word of his. In all the strange situations in which God placed him, he remained calm and silent. He knew the duty of a servant was not to speak but to listen to his master's voice, and that silence is the necessary condition for leading a life of union with God, of close contact with him.

We must not regret not having any words spoken

by Joseph, for the lesson he teaches is precisely the lesson of silence. He knew the Father had confided a secret in trust to him, and the better to keep it so that no slightest inkling of it might leak out, he buried himself in silence. He did not want anyone who saw him to think him other than a simple workman trying to earn his daily bread, so that no sign or word of his might prove an obstacle to the manifestation of the Word.

This quiet self-effacement expressed not only what he considered his utter nothingness before God, but a homage rendered to divine magnificence. He remained breathless in wonder at the sign of what God had done to a poor worthless creature such as he. He felt himself so overwhelmed by glory that only silence could express the depth of his gratitude, his utter annihilation in the presence of this mystery taking place around him. He needed more and more, deeper and deeper silence and recollection in order to meditate on the graces, the mysteries hidden in his heart.

It is a pity about those who see in Joseph the Silent only a poor old-fashioned saint who centuries ago lived and worked as a carpenter in an obscure town, a man who certainly could have no message for us today.

What a mistake they make! It is, on the contrary, really Joseph who teaches our century—not exactly noted for its modesty and submissiveness—the most urgent, most needed lessons. No other model could serve the men of the present time, so wanting in a sense of what makes true greatness. They esteem nothing so much as excitement, noise, striking appearance, quick results. Faith in the advantages of retirement, silence, meditation is lost. Those primordial virtues seem in the eyes of the world to be outworn, outdated, wasted in the up-to-the-minute progress of today.

To the worldly-wise, whatever is opposed to middle class well-being is anathema. Everything must serve to exalt the individual and his supposed rights. The dream of most is that they may make a name for themselves, be distinguished, earn a place in the sun so that the rest of mankind will bow before them.

Joseph teaches us that true greatness consists in serving God and our neighbour; that the only real productiveness springs from a life indifferent to show and glitter, and that the really thrilling exploits are the conscientious and loving accomplishment of one's duties, no matter how humble. They will please God who, seeking nothing but his good pleasure, submit to his design. They will fear but one thing, that of not serving him as faithfully as possible.

Joseph appears before us as the perfect servant, forgetful of self, desiring only his master's glory, ordering his life along lines that will procure that glory. He has no wish to make his actions shine in men's eyes. Within his own soul love burns, love ever attentive to the slightest sign of God's Divine Will.

To remind us of the primacy of the interior and contemplative life, that exterior action should be subordinate to that life, that abnegation must precede and is indispensable to the fruitfulness of that life, is

Joseph's message.

And his final word is that the essential thing is not to appear, but to be; not to bear a title, but to serve; to pass days in doing the will of God and seeking his glory.

As if in Praise of the incomparable holiness, the shining splendour of Joseph's hidden life, these words of Jesus Christ ring out: "I praise you, Father, Lord of heaven and earth, that you did hide these things from the wise and prudent, and did reveal them to the little ones" (Matt 11:25).